LNER 4-6-0s AT WORK

61417

LNER 4-6-0s AT WORK

Geoffrey Hughes

BSc (Econ), C Eng, FIEE

LONDON

IAN ALLAN LTD

Jacket painting by George F. Heiron

Title page:
Sometime in the mid-1950s, Thompson 'B16/3' 4-6-0 No 61417 has plenty of steam to spare as it hauls a lengthy mixed freight off the King Edward Bridge at Newcastle. *Ian Allan Library*

Front endpaper:
'B12/3' 4-6-0 No 61565 takes a Grantham-Peterborough stopping train away from Stoke Tunnel on 2 June 1951. *J. P. Wilson*

Rear endpaper:
The clean, purposeful lines of Thompson's 'B1' 4-6-0 design are displayed to advantage as No 61197 heads a freight train for Fort William near Tyndrum in the 1950s. *P. Ransome-Wallis*

First published 1988

ISBN 0 7110 1712 3

Published by Ian Allan Ltd, Shepperton, Surrey; and printed by Ian Allan Printing Ltd at their works at Coombelands in Runnymede, England

Contents

Foreword

RICHARD HARDY

Geoffrey Hughes is rather a special writer when it comes to the London & North Eastern Railway, in many ways the supreme railway of its time. Here the author has tackled, in his own most interesting style, the story of the LNER 4-6-0 locomotives. It was only when I came to sit down to write this Foreword that I realised that I had worked my passage on every class of locomotive mentioned in the text, with the exception of the 'B6', 'B9', 'B13' and 'B14' classes.

The author writes with the considerable authority gained by close examination of the subject. He has the gift of knowing how to obtain previously unpublished information of great interest, and his deductions on Board and Management policy are sound and revealing. He has, I believe, utilised the services of two retired Chief Mechanical Engineers (CMEs) and no doubt of a Locomotive Running Superintendent (LRS) whose practical knowledge of railways goes back to the Great Northern Railway of 1913. In so doing he has absorbed fascinating and no doubt conflicting information, for rarely, in my experience, did the Departments of the CME and LRS agree with each other. It took time!

Now he has co-opted me, as one who has shared the hardships and pleasures of the footplate and running shed with many men and on a large variety of locomotives, so involving himself up to his neck, in the glorious uncertainty of writing locomotive history! The facts are there when one can find them, but how can those whose lives were so deeply involved with the running of the railway fail now and again to allow their emotions a little rein? Nevertheless Geoffrey Hughes has produced a definitive book, which keeps very much to the point, and so perhaps I can be allowed to add a little icing to the cake, a touch of excitement and emotion, drawing at first-hand on a memory which remains vivid and clear.

During the war, I well remember the North Eastern 'B15s' and 'B16s', which came from Hull, or south across the frontier at Shaftholme Junction. At Doncaster, or in the West Riding or South Yorkshire, they were just 'Geordies', working their freight trains uncomplainingly in a haze of steam from the spindle glands of their outside-admission piston valves. In fact, they were splendid engines, especially the Gresley and Thompson rebuilds, which had inside admission and no steam clouds. 'Foreigners' like us would curse the steam reversing gear on the 'B16s', which would never stay put, but there was a really sound general purpose locomotive, improved by rebuilding when the clutter of eccentrics and big ends on the crank axle was thinned out. The 'B15s' which I fired from Doncaster to Hull steamed marvellously, despite the lack of room in that commodious cab, which, for a start, hampered one's efforts to produce steam. Splashers in the cab, injector control wheels where the fireman would normally sit, and the 'fish and chip' anti-glare shield for the firehole door were a clutter to us, but a North Eastern man would have never given it a thought.

There were very few bad locomotives because the men at the sheds were there to make them go, and so they did. Some burned more coal than others, some had to be coaxed, some were heavy on maintenance, some were rough, and some rode like coaches, but most classes of engines steamed if handled properly and in the way best suited to that particular locomotive. Good steaming was the cornerstone of performance so far as the men were concerned. Occasionally there was a class of locomotive, such as the final version of the Great Northern Atlantic, the 'C1' with piston valves, which defied analysis of any sort, but the Great Central 4-6-0 classes, subject to criticism though they may have been, did their job splendidly. They were 'enginemen's engines', as opposed to the GN Atlantics which could be regarded as 'firemen's engines', so economical were they on the road.

The 'B3s', known as 'Faringdons', criticised by pundits and GN men alike, had been improved out of all recognition when I worked on them. Gresley had authorised the fitting of Caprotti valve gear to four of the class but the remaining two still had piston valves. I doubt if Gresley would have concerned himself greatly with the results of a very minor modification, which took place in the 1930s, not only with Nos 6169 *Lord Faringdon* and 6165 *Valour*, nor only with the four-cylinder 'B7s', but also with the remainder of the Robinson breed fitted with piston valves. Some of his innovations — the Intensifore lubricator and his piston valves most certainly — had been the cause of much profanity, and the introduction of the Doncaster pattern piston valve with a solid head and four narrow rings made a tremendous difference to the performance of the big four-cylinder engines. But there again, the four-cylinder engines had burned their coal when working on long cut-offs, and they were working on long cut-offs because people had been brought up that way. But gradually the scene changed and a growing number of enlightened men began to shorten the cut-off and open the regulator wide, and here again the difference was uncanny.

As for the 'Imminghams', what marvellous engines! They were the workhorses of the West Riding for 25 years, often in the hands of GN men who compared them fairly with their own Atlantics. And their opinion? Good, strong engines — fast, reasonably light on coal and water, comfortable, the firehole a bit high, the horseshoe tender a nuisance because it was not self-trimming, a bit dirty in the cab, indestructible, rarely in trouble of any sort, free running and free for steam. Not a bad verdict! The ride was much better than on an Atlantic, which was an incredibly economical engine, and so the 'Imminghams' burned a bit more coal. Nevertheless, they were the engines which ran all the excursion traffic, including the London jobs which could load up to 14 bogies. Splendid engines! And I have to say that the few trips I made on the 'Sam Fays' were very comfortable and without stress up hill and down dale. They had modified piston valves, too.

'B16/1' No 61430 gives a helping hand to 'K2' 2-6-0 No 61738, the Mogul having stalled on the steeply graded spur between Basford North and Bulwell Common with the 6.15pm ale train from Burton on Trent to York. *P. J. Lynch*

The Great Eastern 'B12s', whether rebuilt or in their original form, were never forgotten by those who worked with them. The first thing to remember is that 75% of those which stayed on the GE section were regular men's engines. I travelled on No 61575 on the last day of steam at Southend. It was Bob Whatling's engine and he was in charge. The same goes for many of the 'B1s' and 'B17s'. Consequently they were objects of pride and attention. Look at the Cambridge 'B17s'. Rough they may have been, but because the maintenance was sound and the crews keen and attentive to their work, the engines were good. Take the Norwich 'B1s'. When they were new, the engines and their crews were inseparable, and although I have never worked at Norwich I can remember the original 1946 allocation as if it were yesterday — Nos 1042 Tallent, 1043 Garnham, 1044 Crowe, 1045 Leman, 1046 Bayles and so on.

In 1986, my wife and I were invited to a Retired Drivers dinner at Ipswich. A very old man, George Dennant, had been brought by his daughter for the first time for many years. He remembered me well enough and kindly, but when I said 'What about old 1561, George, and your "B1" 1252?', we were off in a welter of 1950 reminiscences about the occasion when No 1561 went off the boil and we put things right, so that all was sunshine again. 'His engines' — the 'B12s' — were perfect machines to be treasured. Even their defects were known, and were then watched and anticipated so that they did not develop.

The 'B1' — what a splendid machine, from No 1059, the 'Pride of Ipswich', to the roughest spare engine at Stratford, a real 'bleedin' old Bongo'. How did they compare with a 'Black Five'? The same faults, the same great strengths, much lighter on coal, and water too, but whereas the 'Black Fives' were navvies' engines, the 'B1s' depended a great deal on the skill of that very important man with the shovel — and even then techniques varied between the '1000s' and the '1300s', for example. One day in 1956 we tested No 1372 on the 10.30am to Norwich. She was a spare engine, and had not been steaming. Some Stratford 'improvements' had been made, dictated more by expediency than by scientific application. Had Cecil J. Allen been travelling on the 10.30 that day, we should have been for the high jump. We lost 10min, albeit on a 'Britannia' timing. But coming home, I remember using the poker on starting (to get an immediate white hot fire within a couple of hundred yards) and pushed too much fire forward. Immediately the engine reacted; the fire was bouncing on the firebars under the firehole door, the engine was alive and kicking, we were gaining time and all was well with the world. Theoretically we had done it all wrong, but not for No 1372 nor indeed for Southend's No 1335!

I have written of the practicalities which have been part of my railway life, and which are part of railway folklore. Geoffrey Hughes tells us of so much that is wise, sensible, reliable and historical, and we are bound to differ over details. But it has done me good to think of my old friends again, whether they be 'Fish Engines', 'Imminghams', 'Sam Fays', '1500s', 'B17s', 'B2s' or those two super 4-6-0s Nos 5195 and 5196 which were every bit as good as the Atlantics and less prone to slipping. They have all made history, they have been praised and sworn at, they have been the subject of endless messroom discussion; all of them, all classes, have done their job.

Let Driver Frank Cocksedge of Ipswich have the last word. As a fireman (seniority date 1914), he had Nos 8561 and 2807 as his regular engines, and as a driver, Nos 1569 and 1059, with No 1669 for a considerable period when No 1059 was laid up. He wrote to me in 1966 as follows, after I had unearthed and sent him a special photograph of a 'B12':

'How glad I am of one thing, and it's just this: that I knew and worked on those engines ['B12s'] in their prime — and what work it was too. Yarmouth-London non-stops (and vice versa), 15 bogies on the Norwich, the Antwerp Continental, and the highlight of all, an emigrant special from Ipswich to Liverpool Central, 13 bogies and unassisted over Woodhead. Ah! I think one can say it was a case of good engines, a good mate and good work. I can remember in the 1930s we had a speed up, when the engines were really doing magnificent work, and how thrilled I was to be engaged in it. The attack on the bank at Brentwood with our own engine — I can hear her now. The job was done with every confidence. Boy, it was grand!'

Geoffrey Hughes has taken us into the world of policy and practice, design and management, construction and maintenance of a particular breed of locomotive. I have endeavoured by using Frank Cocksedge's own simple and expressive words to add the final link to the chain, that the steam locomotive depended, every minute, every hour it was in service, on the performance of two men and a host of artisans behind the scenes. A dependence which could rouse passions, even rewrite history. And, finally, the photographs. Each one can tell a story: the majority have not been seen in print before, and will make reading the book a pleasure.

Introduction

Steam locomotives with the 4-6-0 wheel arrangement constituted one of the most popular types of their kind. The story of those which worked on the London & North Eastern Railway has been told before, but not, I feel, quite in the way in which it is related here. Moreover, the search of records which have only recently been made available for inspection throws a good deal more light on less well-known aspects of the work and development of certain classes. This has been supplemented by interviews and correspondence with railwaymen and enthusiasts who were acquainted with many of the engines concerned when they were hard at work in revenue-earning service, not only for the LNER but also for its predecessors and successors.

I am particularly grateful to Dick Hardy — writing as one with steam in his blood! — for contributing the Foreword, and to J. F. Harrison OBE and T. C. B. Miller MBE, both stalwarts in the Gresley tradition, for guidance on many technical matters. In assembling the material I owe a great debt of gratitude to John F. Clay for putting at my disposal his own store of information, as well as providing unstinted help throughout the compilation of this book. Others to whom I am indebted include Willie Yeadon, for his wide-ranging advice, and Allan Brown, Lyn Brooks, Geoff Goslin, Bernard Harding, Ken Hoole, David Jackson, Eric Neve and Owen Russell for assistance in their own specialised fields.

Source material has been found in the archives of the Public Record Office, the National Railway Museum, the Institution of Mechanical Engineers and the Chartered Institute of Transport; in particular investigations, I have been assisted by the librarians of the Mitchell Library and the University of Glasgow, and the Greater Manchester Museum of Science and Industry.

It is believed that the great majority of photographs are published here for the first time, and only a small number with particular historical interest are repeated. Photographic libraries have been researched to find a suitable cross-section of illustrations, including those of the National Railway Museum, Rail Archive Stephenson and Real Photos, as well as the collections of a number of Railway Societies and individuals. The choice of photographs of BR subjects is, of course, much wider than those of the LNER period, simply because the standard of equipment available to the amateur has been so much higher in postwar days. This is why most of the studies of the 'B1s', for instance, are taken after 1947 — but, of course, most of their work was performed during this period anyway. One aspect which has defied adequate coverage is the work of the 'B12s' on ambulance trains during the war, but this is perhaps to be expected, having regard to the restrictions on travel during that period.

There are several books and journals available to the enthusiast who wishes to delve more deeply into the history and details of the locomotives described in this book. Of particular interest is the multi-part series *Locomotives of the LNER*, published by the Railway Correspondence and Travel Society, as well as the monthly issues and files of the *Railway Gazette*, the *Railway Magazine* and *Railway World*. John Clay's earlier book on the subject, the *LNER 4-6-0 Classes* (Ian Allan Ltd), written in collaboration with Joe Cliffe, goes deeper into certain aspects of individual performance than is possible in the present volume. Also, the specialist railway societies — the Gresley Society, the LNER Study Group, the Great Central Railway Society, the Great Eastern Railway Society, the Great Northern Railway Society, the North Eastern Railway Association and others — offer the enthusiast further opportunities to investigate still further the development of his favourite breed of steam locomotive. Finally, I must express my appreciation of the work put in by my wife, Mary, in reading and commenting on successive drafts, and for assistance in typing draft and final texts.

Geoffrey Hughes

Chorley Wood
May 1987

1

The 4-6-0 Type

The 4-6-0 has proved to be one of the most generally useful locomotive types in the entire history of steam, having been employed in all parts of the world on all kinds of duty. The first 4-6-0s were introduced in the United States, as an extended and enlarged version of the 4-4-0, with the additional advantage of permitting reduction of the load on individual axles, so enabling lightweight track and underbridges to support an increased total weight.

The first 4-6-0s to be built in Britain were turned out by Dübs and Co of Glasgow in 1880 for the Indian State Railways, but none were seen in traffic on a British railway until 1894, when the Highland Railway introduced a class with 5ft 3in driving wheels, mainly for freight traffic. On their native line, they were dubbed the 'Big Goods', but further afield were known as the 'Jones Goods' after David Jones, who was responsible for their design. They were used on occasion to haul passenger trains, and one of the class has been preserved in the Glasgow Museum of Transport. The Great Western Railway followed suit in 1896 with another pioneer goods engine, No 36, with 4ft 6in wheels and double frames. However, by the turn of the century requirements for more powerful passenger engines led locomotive engineers to consider how best to improve on the still widely used but by then obsolescent single-wheelers, 2-4-0s and small-boilered 4-4-0s. However, the 4-6-0 was only one option, and many designers were reluctant to take the step forward into the six-coupled era — after all, it was not many years since the view had been expressed that coupled wheels were a hindrance to speed. So, alternative arrangements were given serious consideration, such as enlarging the well-tried 4-4-0, or adding a trailing axle to give a 4-4-2 (Atlantic) wheel arrangement. Of the LNER constituent companies, the Great Northern and North British (NBR) opted for Atlantics, whilst the Great North of Scotland, limited by sparse traffic and lightweight track, built nothing larger than low powered 4-4-0s. On the other hand, the Great Central (GCR) and the North Eastern (NER) experimented with all three options, the NER indeed being the first in the field so far as Britain was concerned in introducing a passenger version of the 4-6-0, in 1899. The GCR were also early in bringing out a 4-6-0, one similar to that of the NER appearing in 1902, but whilst both companies developed further versions of the type, some of impressive proportions, none achieved the undisputed position of being the first choice for front-line passenger work, and four-coupled engines were to be seen on most of the best GCR and NER expresses until the Grouping, and after. Only the Great Eastern took a firm decision to employ 4-6-0s on these duties as a matter of course; S. D. Holden's '1500' class being one of the very few inside-cylindered examples of the type to achieve success.

Later developments in the USA tended to favour a 4-6-2 (Pacific) design, rather than the option of extending the coupled wheelbase further into a 4-8-0, although a number of examples of this type were built. The reason was that the firebox of a 4-6-0 or 4-8-0 was restricted in width to the space between the coupled wheels, and in depth by the rear coupled axles, unless the driving wheels were of comparatively small diameter. On the other hand the greater space available over the trailing wheels of a 4-6-2 permitted a longer and deeper firebox, or alternatively a wider one, with more of the grate within easy reach of the firehole. In the final year before Grouping, both the Great Northern and the North Eastern produced 4-6-2 designs, although of widely differing characteristics.

It is of interest to consider the reasoning behind the NBR decision to concentrate on the Atlantic rather than the 4-6-0 type, as their Scottish counterparts had done. In 1910 the matter was taken as far as trials on the LNWR main line north of Preston, between No 881 *Borderer* and the 'Experiment' class

Facing page, right and below right: The first three British designs of large-wheeled 4-6-0s, all with outside cylinders and inside valve gear. Wilson Worsdell led the way with his 'S1' class, introduced on the North Eastern Railway in 1900 and illustrated here by No 2113 (facing page). This was followed in 1902 by GWR No 100 (right), and in 1903 by the Great Central '8G' class of J. G. Robinson (below right), of which No 196 was one of the only two built.
Bucknall Collection; Ian Allan Library; LPC (A4498)

No 1483 *Redgauntlet*. No difference in timekeeping was noted, but the Atlantic was said to have been heavier on coal. The intention had been to compare the two engines on the Waverley route between Carlisle and Edinburgh, but this was not possible as the chimney of the LNWR engine was too high for some of the overbridges. Nevertheless, despite the inconclusive results, the 4-4-2 arrangement was retained on the basis that its more flexible wheelbase took the curves of the Waverley route better than a 4-6-0 would have done.

One of the earliest decisions on locomotive policy taken by the LNER Board was that H. N. Gresley's Pacifics were to be standardised as the main source of passenger motive power on the East Coast route. In this use of Pacifics the LNER was years ahead of the LMS and the Southern, which did not introduce Pacifics until 1932 and 1941 respectively — and, in the case of the Southern, only after Gresley's one-time Assistant, O. V. S. Bulleid, had been appointed Chief Mechanical Engineer (CME). Moreover, no more than 51 Pacifics were built to LMS designs, this company relying on 4-6-0s for all but the heaviest and fastest services, whereas almost eight times this number of LNER 4-6-2s and 2-6-2s were built. The Great Western of course employed the most powerful 4-6-0s in the country, and after their unsatisfactory experience with *The Great Bear* showed no inclination towards a Pacific design. The reason for the LNER preference for Pacifics was Gresley's clear decision, based on experience with the Great Northern Atlantics and observation of the Pennsylvania Railroad 'K4s' class, that a large boiler and wide firebox formed the best combination for effective steam raising when working heavy loads over long distances. This policy was to be extended during his time as CME of the LNER, indeed his liking for the wide firebox and consequent trailing axle was seen in his comparatively small locomotive, the 'V4' 2-6-2. The effect of the LNER 'Big Engine' policy was that trains which on that line were hauled by Pacifics or 2-6-2s would have been in the hands of 'Royal Scot' 4-6-0s on the LMS or 'Castles' on the Great Western.

This is not to say however that the LNER neglected the 4-6-0 type, as two classes were built in quantity to post-Grouping designs. Both were of medium power, the first, the 'B17', being introduced in 1928, whilst the second, Edward Thompson's 'B1', must be regarded as one of the most successful of British general-purpose 4-6-0s. Moreover, Gresley instituted radical improvements to the Great Eastern, and the final North Eastern, classes — work which was continued by Thompson. Gresley is also believed to have given serious consideration to a larger 4-6-0, the equivalent in power output of a 'Castle', as a possible complement to his 'V2' 2-6-2s of the later 1930s. However, this would have been with some reluctance on his part, in view of his preference for the wide Wootten type of firebox.

It will be seen, then, that apart from the Great Eastern section, 4-6-0s were only infrequently used for the best expresses on the LNER system, either before or after the Grouping, but for contrasting reasons: the constituent companies employed four-coupled locomotives, in some cases *smaller* dimensionally than 4-6-0s on the same line, whilst in LNER days the preference was for engines *larger* than most other contemporary 4-6-0s. Nevertheless, there are no fewer than 16 main classes to be considered in this survey of LNER 4-6-0s at work, as well as a number of sub-classes introduced as a result of rebuilding; altogether they compose a rich assortment of locomotive design. A total of 315 were built to pre-Grouping specifications 73 were of the Gresley 'B17' class, and there were 410 'B1s'. In aggregate, 798 4-6-0s were in LNER or BR service, although not all at the same time, as many of the older ones had been withdrawn by the time the first 'B1' made its appearance — this design in any case being intended as the replacement for many obsolete classes due for withdrawal. The highest number in any year was in fact 605, in 1952, five years after the demise of the LNER. This number was achieved mainly by the delivery of large numbers of newly built 'B1s' in post-Nationalisation years, whilst most of the 'B12s', 'B16s' and 'B17s' and their rebuilds still remained in service. So, in looking at LNER 4-6-0s we are surveying a variety of designs which spanned the years from 1899 until the last was withdrawn in 1966; happily, two 'B1s' and a 'B12/3' have been preserved. Whilst no LNER 4-6-0 qualified for a BR Power Classification higher than 6MT, in their time and as far as their capabilities permitted, they handled the widest range of traffic from pick-up goods to passenger expresses.

2

North Eastern 4-6-0s

The North Eastern Railway produced four designs of 4-6-0, totalling 135 locomotives in all, and classified 'S', 'S1', 'S2' and 'S3' on that railway, the LNER classifications being 'B13', 'B14', 'B15' and 'B16' respectively. Whilst there was much in common to all four designs, they did not form a coherent series in which each subsequent class was developed from the one before; rather they fell into two groups — the 'S' and 'S1', which were very similar except for their coupled wheel dimensions, and were intended for express working north and south of Newcastle respectively, and the 'S2' and 'S3', which were introduced specifically for mixed traffic working. The first 'S', No 2001, was completed at Gateshead in 1899 and was the pioneer of the long line of British 4-6-0s which handled the bulk of long distance passenger working right up to the end of steam.

These new 4-6-0s were intended to haul the heaviest trains between Newcastle and Edinburgh, and to assist in hill climbing were provided with driving wheels of the relatively small diameter, for passenger engines, of 6ft 1¼in. The previous engines to be built for this work were the 'Q' 4-4-0s, of which 30 came out in 1896-97; with driving wheels 1ft larger, their tractive effort was 14,974lb. That of the 'S' was half as much again, and with a corresponding increase in heating surface and adhesive weight, the new engines were expected to achieve good results.

The North Eastern management were rightly proud of their new acquisitions, which were the most powerful engines in Britain at the time; one of the first batch to be built, No 2006, was sent to the Paris Exhibition of 1900, where it was awarded a gold medal. Interestingly, another British exhibit was the Midland Railway single-wheeler No 2601 *Princess of Wales*, the two representing the commencement of one era and the end of another. One wonders what the Midland hoped to achieve by showing such an example of obsolescent practice, splendid though it appeared in its livery of crimson lake and polished brass. However, the prestige associated with the award of the gold medal was somewhat diminished by the paucity of exhibits, only two other locomotives — the Great Eastern 4-4-0 *Claud Hamilton* and the LNWR compound *La France* — having been sent by railways in Britain.

The first 10 'S' class locomotives were put to work on the Edinburgh road without delay, the NER providing the motive power for through trains to avoid changing engines at the frontier point at Berwick. In the aftermath of the race to Aberdeen, trains had become significantly heavier, some with the addition of restaurant car facilities, and this had led to double-heading, a practice which the new 4-6-0s were intended to eliminate. As well as providing these 6ft 1¼in engines to work north of Newcastle, Wilson Worsdell, the NER Locomotive Superintendent, introduced 4-6-0s on the easier section of the East Coast main line between York and Newcastle, a 6ft 8¼in version of the 'S' emerging from Gateshead at the end of 1900, the latter being classified 'S1'. It was soon discovered that the difference in driving wheel diameter did not lead to any distinguishable variation in the performance of the two classes, and before long they were used indiscriminately between York and Edinburgh. Only five 'S1s' were built, all at Gateshead.

At the same time as the 'S' class was being developed, Wilson Worsdell brought out an enlargement of the 'Q' class, this being known as the 'R' class, with a 30% increase in tractive effort over the earlier engines. The order of class letters indicates that in the drawing office the 4-4-0 had originally been given priority over

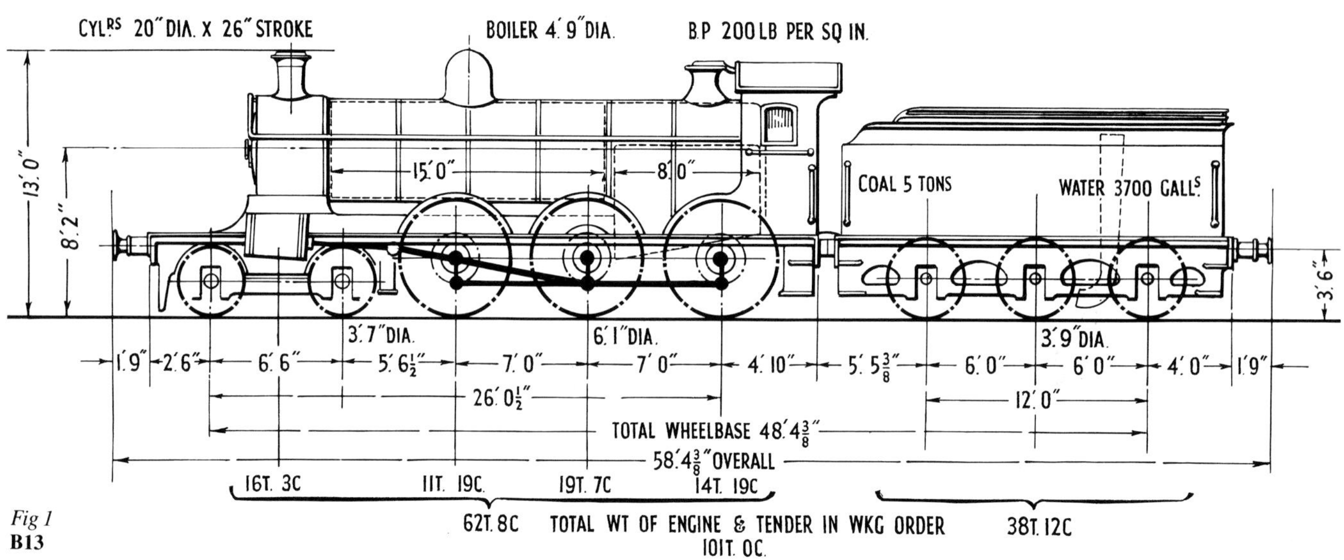

Fig 1
B13

the 4-6-0, whereas in the event the first 'S' was turned out a few weeks before the first 'R'; however, possibly because of construction problems with the new, larger, engines, the first 10 'Rs' were completed in the same period as only six 'Ss', the two classes being built concurrently. If Worsdell had fully intended the 4-6-0s to work the heaviest duties, it is not clear why he should have built an enlarged version of his 4-4-0s as well. Perhaps he was not completely assured of the capabilities of his 4-6-0s, and wanted to ensure that he had some powerful 4-4-0s to fall back upon if necessary. He had in fact made a significant step forward in British locomotive design, by introducing a six-coupled engine with outside cylinders driving on to the centre axle, for fast passenger work. In this he was over a year ahead of G. J. Churchward, who (whilst William Dean was still nominally in charge of Great Western locomotive development) had built No 100, the forerunner of the 'Saint' class, in 1902.

In the event, however, Worsdell's new 4-6-0s did not live up to expectations, and were unable to develop the power hoped for by their designer. The reasons for this are not altogether clear, but would seem to lie in the inability of the boiler to generate sufficient steam for the 20in×26in cylinders. Perhaps a larger grate would have been beneficial — at 23sq ft it was in fact slightly smaller than that of the contemporary Midland single — and an important contributory factor was said to lie in the shallowness of the grate, which tended to restrict the supply of air to the fire if the fireman was too heavy with the shovel. Moreover, anxiety about overheating when working hard led to prudence on the part of the driver. As an example of contemporary performance by an 'S' class locomotive, one took 155min to cover the 124.4 miles between Newcastle and Edinburgh, with a stop at Berwick, when hauling the 'Flying Scotsman', the train consisting of a string of six-wheeled vehicles totalling 352 tons tare. Delay had been caused by a goods train in the early stages of the run, but no more than 65mph was achieved down Cockburnspath Bank.

On the other hand, the 'R' 4-4-0s steamed well and were liked by their crews, and as a result supplanted the 4-6-0s from the hardest tasks. Indeed, the first of the 'Rs', No 2011, ran a double turn on six days a week from Newcastle to Edinburgh and back, and then to Leeds and back, for almost the first two years of its life. However, Charles Rous-Marten, a well known observer of those days, recorded a number of runs with 'S1s' which demonstrated that a 4-6-0 was not inhibited from high speeds by the coupling of three pairs of wheels. The fastest of these was with a 260-ton train from Darlington to a signal stop just outside York, in which the 43.9 miles occupied no more than 40min 51sec, at an average of 64.5mph, and with a maximum speed of 72mph. On another occasion the 66.9 miles from Newcastle to Berwick took no more than 66min 24sec with 300 tons. Top speed was 80mph, and a minimum of 52½mph was claimed up the 1 in 170 of Longhoughton Bank.

Wilson Worsdell visited the United States in 1901, and returned imbued with the capabilities of the Atlantic type, which was then a popular alternative to the 4-6-0 on American railways. In particular he was impressed by the achievements of the 4-4-2s on the Reading Railroad, whose 'Atlantic City Fliers' were the fastest trains in the world at the time. Moreover, the North Eastern's southern partner, the Great Northern, was building Atlantics, and these could often be seen at York. Consequently Worsdell turned his back on the development of 4-6-0s for fast passenger work, and concentrated on the 4-4-2 instead, building 10 large Atlantics of the 'V' class at Gateshead in 1903-04, followed by two similar, but compound, versions, two years later. For the next eight years, until Raven's still larger 'Z' class Atlantics came on the scene, the 4-4-2s and the 'R' 4-4-0s between them handled the majority of the best trains on the North Eastern system, the 4-6-0s being increasingly used on fast goods services.

Towards the end of 1906, a series of tests were carried out between Newcastle and York with the 'S' and 'S1' classes, as well as the later 'V' and '4CC' Compound Atlantics. In the last trip by the 'S1', No 2114, hauling the 1.52pm down non-stop with 11 coaches weighing 365 tons, the 80.1 miles were run at an average

Below:
'B13' No 2006 is seen in the paint shop yard at Darlington, in readiness for the Centenary Parade on 2 July 1925. The engine is little different in appearance to the day in 1900 when it was awarded a Gold Medal at the Paris Exhibition; replicas of the medal are fixed to the centre splashers. The main outward indication that the engine had been rebuilt with piston valves and superheater is a short extension of the smokebox. In addition, the original brass-capped chimney has been replaced by a plain one with a capuchon. *BR*

speed of 49.2mph compared with the 52.5mph called for by the schedule. The maximum speed was 71mph at Chester-le-Street and Birtley, with a low of 33mph through Durham; boiler pressure was maintained at 175lb/sq in. The Compound Atlantic was seen as the best performer, and the conclusion was that if the 'R' was graded as 100, the 'S1' would be 105 and the '4CC' 145. However, the 'S1' was reported to be in very good condition, and consequently its average performance should be taken as no more than equal to that of the 'R'. These Worsdell designs were produced at a time when fundamental changes in steam valve design were under consideration. The first eight 'Ss' had conventional slide valves, but the contemporary 'R' 4-4-0s were provided with piston valves, as were the remainder of 'Ss' and the 'S1s'. Later, all were to have piston valves.

As an advanced design, it is not surprising that the 'S' and 'S1' classes gave rise to a number of minor problems. At first, anxiety over their ability to circumvent tight curves led to the omission of flanges on the centre pair of coupled wheels, but these were soon replaced by flanged wheels. The new engines were longer than any others in NER stock, and this raised the question of their accommodation on the 50ft turntables then in use at the major depots. The NER had long shown consideration for their enginemen by the provision of a substantial cab with two side windows, but this could not be incorporated in the new engines without leading to excessive overall length. Consequently, the first examples were turned out with a cab shortened by 2ft; the tender was also reduced in length. However, there was a reaction by the footplate crews to the retrograde step of providing their latest locomotives with smaller cabs than those to which they were accustomed, and consequently not only were later engines given normal cabs, but within a couple of years the original small ones had been replaced. Until larger turntables were installed, turning was achieved on triangular sections of track, although at some operational disadvantage.

With the successful performance on passenger trains of the 'R' 4-4-0s and 'V' 4-4-2s, the 'S' 4-6-0s became the first large locomotives in Great Britain to be used as a truly mixed traffic type. In this they achieved a new role by accident, but one in which they came to be regarded so highly that further construction of the 'S' class took place, 10 more being built in 1906 and another 20 in 1908-09, all at Gateshead. They were allotted vacant numbers in the NER locomotive register, all except one being in the 700 series. (It is interesting to note that the numbers of the first six to be built, Nos 2001 to 2006, were later appropriated for the renowned *Cock o' the North* and its five companions, but this was after the 4-6-0s concerned had been withdrawn for scrapping.) The later batches differed in appearance from the originals in that whereas the earlier engines had been provided with wide splashers, the last 20 were given a markedly different style, with narrow splashers and a wide box-like structure to contain the coupling rods.

In their later years, including the post-Grouping period, the 'S' and 'S1' classes continued in mixed traffic employment, such as fish and other perishable workings, and excursion and secondary passenger trains, but they were gradually replaced on important jobs by more modern locomotives. However, No 2006, the Paris Exhibition engine, was to be in the public eye once more when it took part in the parade of rolling stock in the Stockton & Darlington Centenary celebrations in 1925. For this important occasion it was painted in LNER green and made an impressive display, with highly polished brasswork and tall boiler mountings emphasising its well balanced proportions.

The first of the 'S' class to be withdrawn was No 2004, in August 1928; the 'S1s' went in 1929-31 and all but one of the 'S' class had gone by the end of 1938. The exception was No 761, which was transferred to service stock to act as a counter-pressure locomotive in conjunction with the dynamometer car, its role being to absorb the energy generated by the engine under test. It operated by working normally whilst the locomotive being tested was accelerating, but once the required speed was reached the counter-pressure locomotive was put into reverse, water being admitted to the cylinders and pumped against the pressure in the boiler. Originally No 756 was selected for this job, but the conversion was not a success. This engine was

Bottom left:
No 2002 is seen as NER Class S in workshop grey for photographic purposes, soon after having been completed at Gateshead in 1899. A notable feature is the small single-window cab which was replaced after two years by the normal pattern one.
LPC/Ian Allan Library (A2360)

Left:
Soon after commencing service, No 2002 is seen at Newcastle Central station. Note the shorter smokebox, compared with that of No 2006 after superheating, and the North Eastern Railway armorial device on the centre splasher. *Ian Allan Library*

scrapped, and No 761, also due for withdrawal, was given a general repair at Darlington, special instructions having been given that the pistons should be a good fit in the cylinders. It was first used in a test in January 1935, when it was said to have performed very satisfactorily, 1,500hp being absorbed for 16 miles and 1,850hp for about a mile, without overheating. With the completion after Nationalisation of the Rugby Testing Plant, the engine was moved there but does not appear to have been utilised; it was eventually scrapped in 1951.

As the 'S' class had so successfully demonstrated the value of powerful mixed traffic engines, yet another 10 were authorised in 1911, but by then V. R. Raven had succeeded Worsdell and substituted his own design, known as the 'S2' class, specifically for these duties. The main difference from the 'S' class was an increase in boiler diameter from 4ft 9in to 5ft 6in, and 30% more heating surface; grate area, cylinders and wheel diameter were unchanged. It seems strange that no increase was made in grate area to meet the demands of the larger boiler, and as a result the class were said to run short of steam and not be favourites with the enginemen. Even so, they possessed a useful turn of speed, one reaching 74mph at the foot of the gentle descent before Beningbrough, and managing the 44.1 miles between Darlington and York in 45¾min net with 350 tons behind the tender. The first seven used saturated steam, but by that time the virtues of superheating were becoming appreciated, and those subsequently built were fitted with superheaters. Apart from the larger boiler, their external lineaments were similar to those of the later members of the 'S' class, but with lower boiler mountings; also, Ramsbottom safety valves within a brass trumpet gave way to Ross pop pattern mounted on a platform. Twenty 'S2s' were built at Darlington between December 1911 and March 1913, Gateshead works having ceased to manufacture locomotives in 1910. The class took vacant numbers between 782 and 825, and the first withdrawals took place in 1937, although most lasted until just after World War 2.

The last of the class to enter traffic, No 825, was one of two Raven locomotives to be equipped experimentally with Stumpf 'Uniflow' cylinders, the other being a 'Z' Atlantic; both engines were noted for their noisy exhaust, likened to that of a motor cycle without a silencer. The principle of this system, sometimes found in stationary engines, is for the flow of steam to be maintained in one direction only, with the theoretical advantage of lower back-pressure and less condensation, which otherwise arises from the cooling of the ports and cylinder walls by exhaust steam. In practice this required a cylinder twice as long as normal, steam being admitted to each end alternately, and exhausted at the centre. The Stumpf engines were said to use less coal than their conventional counterparts, but the results were inconclusive and they were eventually rebuilt with normal cylinders.

Vincent Raven, even whilst Assistant to Wilson Worsdell, was developing his predilection for three-cylinder propulsion, the first NER design to be produced with this feature being the 'X' class 4-8-0T, 10 of which were built in 1909-10. After Raven had succeeded Worsdell as Chief Mechanical Engineer in 1910, further three-cylinder designs were seen in the 'Y' class 4-6-2T, 'Z' class 4-4-2 and 'D' class 4-4-4T. With the intervention of World War 1, no further developments took place until 1919, when the need for additional 4-6-0 mixed traffic locomotives provided the opportunity for an updated design of the 'S2' to be prepared, with three cylinders instead of two. The result was the 'S3', a substantially more powerful locomotive than its predecessors, with 5ft 8in coupled wheels, 1,958sq ft of heating surface, including superheater, and a grate area increased to 27sq ft; the tractive effort was as high as 30,032lb, similar to that of the contemporary Gresley 'K3' 2-6-0s. No fewer than 70 of the new class were built, all at Darlington, betwen 1919 and 1924, the final 15 resulting from a NER recommendation endorsed by the LNER Locomotive Committee during the first year of the Grouping. As well as being more powerful than the earlier NER 4-6-0s the 'S3s' were also more reliable, and consequently popular with their crews. They were employed on all NER main lines, primarily on fast freight trains, but also as a valuable back-up for secondary passenger and excursion workings.

Like Raven's other three-cylinder designs, in which separate Stephenson's link motion was provided for each cylinder, the 'S3s' suffered from mechanical congestion arising from the amount of machinery between the frames. All three cylinders drove on to the leading coupled axle, and in consequence there were six eccentrics rotating in close proximity to each other in addition to the cranked driving axle — a situation which must have made the carrying out of adjustments far from easy. Little thought appears to have been given by the Darlington design office to alleviate the maintenance problems introduced

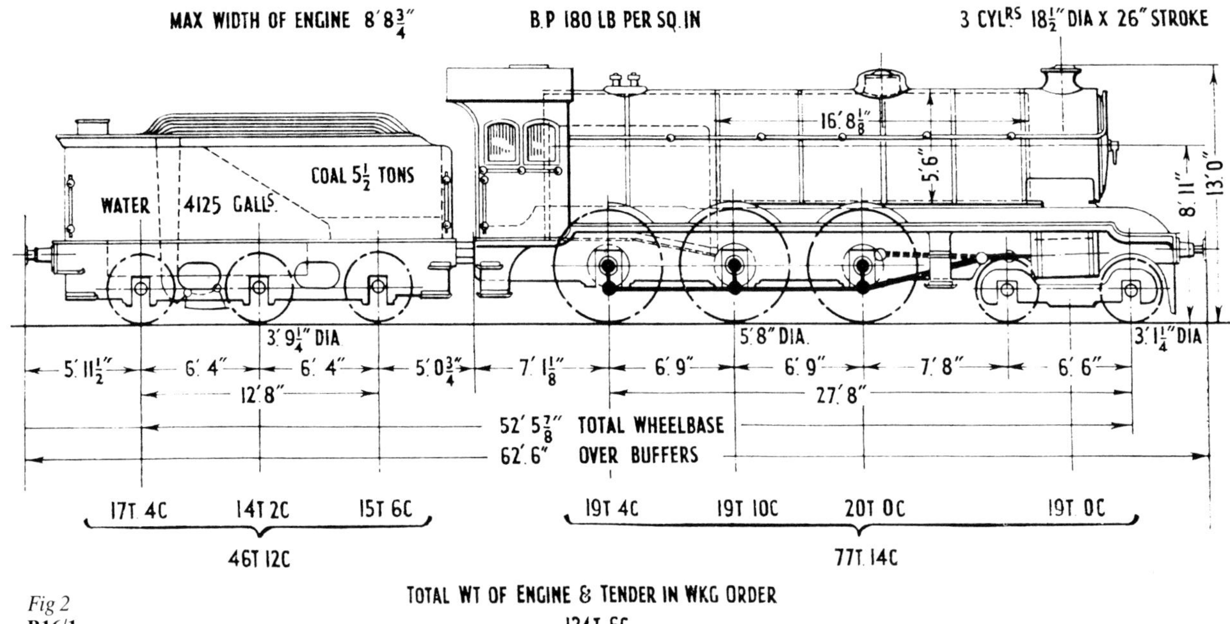

Fig 2
B16/1

by this particular variant of the three-cylinder configuration; however, it did possess the advantage, important in many people's minds in those days, of enabling the provision of a clean external outline. The Raven style was in contrast to Gresley's attitude towards three-cylinder drive, in which the motion for the centre valve spindle was derived from that of the outside valves, so that only the connecting rod to the driving axle was located within the frames, making access so much easier.

Raven had the opportunity to defend his reasoning when, in 1925, as President of the Institution of Mechanical Engineers, he reiterated his views on locomotive valve gear. The occasion was the Summer Meeting of the Institution, at which Gresley read an important paper entitled 'Three-Cylinder High Pressure Locomotives', setting out in detail the reasons for his preference for this method of propulsion. At the end of the discussion Raven expressed his general agreement in principle with Gresley's reasoning, but concluded that as he believed in simplicity he had always used three sets of Stephenson valve gear, saying that 'If I went back to rail work today I would do the same again'.

With the appointment of Gresley as Chief Mechanical Engineer of the LNER group, the Great Northern 2-6-0 (LNER 'K3') was adopted as the standard heavy mixed traffic class, and was turned out in large numbers, commencing with a sequence of 60 built at Darlington in 1924-25. Despite the difference in driving technique, and the roughness in riding compared with the native 4-6-0s — due in part to the pony truck and shorter wheelbase — the new 'K3s' were stationed in the North Eastern Area in increasing numbers right from the date they were first turned out, and there is no strong evidence of hostility towards them on the part of the NER enginemen. They were put to work on the same duties as the 'S3s' (now reclassified 'B16'), the only stipulation by the local operating authorities apparently being that they should be numbered within the North Eastern range of running numbers.

In LNER days, the position of Mechanical Engineer Darlington — that is, Gresley's Assistant in the North Eastern Area — was held by A. C. Stamer, who, in view of his seniority, carried the title of Assistant Chief Mechanical Engineer. Stamer had been Raven's erstwhile assistant, and retired at the end of 1933, being succeeded by Edward Thompson, with the title of Mechanical Engineer, North Eastern Area — the position of Assistant Chief being allowed to lapse. Thompson had been in the similar position at Stratford, and before then Carriage & Wagon Works Manager for the North Eastern Area. On the advice of these engineers, Gresley, with Board approval, had authorised the conversion of the 'D' class 4-4-4T to a 4-6-2T, but with the retention of the three-cylinder drive. Consideration was also given to the reconstruction of a number of the 'Z' (now 'C7') Atlantics and 'B16' 4-6-0s on Gresley lines with outside Walschaerts valve gear and derived motion for the inside valves. The proposals for the 'C7s' were cancelled in view of the number of Pacifics entering service, but those for the 'B16s' were put into effect. At the same time the running plate was raised to expose the coupled wheels, and high window cabs were provided. The new cylinders were cast in one piece together with the smokebox saddle, and the valve movements redesigned with increased travel, in accordance with experience gained with other classes subjected to this treatment; the valve chambers were slightly increased in diameter from 8⅞in to 9in. Seven of the class were rebuilt in this way, the first in 1937. After Thompson had succeeded Gresley as CME in 1941, he continued the rebuilding but altered the style to conform to his own principles, three separate sets of Walschaerts valve gear being provided as in his Pacific designs. It must have been thought that he would have considered a more drastic rebuilding, with only two cylinders, as he had done with other classes, but this was not to be the case, nor did he provide his rebuilds with his standard boiler, the diagram 100A. The reason for this appears to lie with the slightly closer positioning of the frames in this Darlington design than was the case in Doncaster practice, and it was not possible to overcome this and so allow the fitting of the standard boiler. However, a modernisation of the 'B16' boiler layout had been completed in 1939, and new boilers to this specification were fitted to a number of the class when replacements were needed, as well as to the Thompson rebuilds. The LNER gave the amended classification of 'B16/2' to the Gresley, and 'B16/3' to the Thompson rebuilds, of which there were 17. The originals became 'B16/1'.

It may be considered surprising that Thompson persisted with the monobloc cylinder casting, which was a feature of the 'B16/2s', but which had to be scrapped and replaced if one

Above and left:
No 752 was one of the last batch of 'B13s' built at Gateshead in 1908-09. It retained its Ramsbottom safety valves inside a brass trumpet-shaped cover after superheating in 1920, but these were later changed to Ross pop type with a shortened cover. This engine is seen heading a down mixed goods train near York, c1922 (above), whilst in 1929 it is in charge of a solitary parcels van, travelling south near Goswick (left).
Bucknall Collection/Ian Allan Library; L&GRP, courtesy David & Charles (20691)

cylinder became cracked, but evidently this was of a sufficiently infrequent occurrence not to give rise to concern. The same constructional method applied to the 'V2s', but in this case when, under BR auspices, the class was nearing the end of its life, separate cylinders and outside steam pipes were provided whenever a cylinder needed replacement. Earlier, whilst Thompson was still at Darlington, improvements had been made to the wheel bearings of the 'B16s', and in addition mechanical lubrication was provided and changes made to the balancing of the coupled wheels, in attempts to obtain still greater reliability.

There was always a heavy concentration of 'B16s' at York, and indeed the whole class was stationed there between 1943 and 1949, apart from short-term loans to other sheds. After Nationalisation they were often seen away from the North Eastern area, sometimes on a working to King's Cross in place of a rostered 'V2'. In the later 1950s they appeared more often on passenger workings, particularly at holiday times, such as the Filey Holiday Camp trains, or even the 'Scarborough Flier' between York and Scarborough. There seems to have been little preference between the three varieties of the class.

The first 'B16' to be withdrawn was No 925, damaged beyond repair in the air raid on York on 29 April 1942, in which 'A4' Pacific No 4469 *Sir Ralph Wedgwood* was also destroyed. Otherwise, the class lasted almost until the end of steam in the northeast, one being withdrawn in 1958 and the others following over the next few years until all had gone by 1964. As with most 'maid of all work' mixed traffic locomotives, the 'B16s' carried out their duties without reaching the headlines, an exception being No 934. This achieved a moment of glory in 1925, when it accompanied 'B13' No 2006 in the Stockton & Darlington Centenary Parade.

When the first NER 4-6-0, No 2001, made its appearance in 1899, it was accorded passenger green livery, fully lined out, and this continued to be the case with the 'Ss' and 'S1s' until just before World War 1, when they were painted black, although splendidly lined out in white, red and gold. In time this was replaced by the simpler single red lining later adopted by the LNER, except that the 'S1s', with 6ft 8¼in driving wheels, qualified for LNER express passenger livery and hence appeared in apple green, lined out in black edged with white, until they were withdrawn. The 'S2s' and 'S3s', never intended primarily as express engines, were painted black for the whole of their lives. A few of the former class (later 'B15') and all the latter ('B16'), together with the counter-pressure locomotive, survived to be renumbered under the postwar LNER scheme. The 'B15s' took numbers in the 1300s and the 'B16s' in the 1400s, but following the influx of new 'B1s' the surviving 'B15s' took Nos 1691 to 1698, and the first 10 'B16s' went to the end of their group, which then occupied Nos 61410 to 61468 in the BR lists. The counter-pressure locomotive became BR No 61699.

This picture and below:
Two other members of the last batch of 'B13s', at the beginning and end of their respective careers. No 753, with gleaming brasswork, is seen heading an up express at Low Fell c1910, while No 756, in plain black, is seen at Bridlington in 1930 with a Scarborough train of LMS stock.
R. J. Purves/Gresley Society Collection; T. E. Rounthwaite

Above:
The 'S1s' were originally intended to work express passenger trains on the NER main line between Newcastle and York. Here No 2112 is seen in charge of a down express at Beningbrough, c1905. The leading coaches are East Coast Joint Stock. *LPC/Ian Allan Library (7673)*

Below:
'B14' No 2115, seen here on Scottish metals at Longniddry in 1923. North Eastern locomotives regularly worked passenger trains through to Edinburgh, to avoid changing engines at Berwick.
L&GRP, courtesy David & Charles (20188)

Above left:
The 'B15s' were a true mixed traffic class, and were used on a variety of services. The first to be built, No 782, is seen in company with a Midland Railway van outside Newcastle Central on 19 July 1913.
Bucknall Collection/Ian Allan Library

Left:
Through trains from the Midlands and the Northwest were often seen at York. Here, an LMS excursion is leaving for Scarborough, around 1933, in the charge of 'B15' No 813. *Real Photos (T6798)*

Above:
The date of this photograph is uncertain, but is believed to be c1926. 'B15' No 820 is seen on a working on which a Great Central 'O4' would have been expected — a train of loaded coal wagons emerging from the western portal of the Woodhead tunnel. *Real Photos (T5537)*

Below:
No 820 is seen again in a more familiar role, heading an up van train near Goswick in 1929. This engine was the last of its class to be withdrawn, at the end of 1947, by which time it had been renumbered 1696.
L&GRP, courtesy David & Charles (20690)

Right:
No 825 was completed in March 1913, the last 'B15' to be built. It was fitted from new with the German Stumpf cylinder arrangement, which materially altered the engine's appearance. Note the additional handrail necessitated by the high running plate. *Real Photos (W1845)*

Below:
The workmanlike lines of the three-cylinder 'B16s' are well brought out in this photograph of No 2376 on the turntable at the north end of Nottingham Victoria, with the portal of Mansfield Road tunnel in the background, around 1927. Note the continuing use of the NER classification 'S3' on the buffer beam. Later, this mode of denoting an engine's class was adopted throughout the LNER system. *T. G. Hepburn/ Rail Archive Stephenson*

Above:
On 28 August 1960, a year before its withdrawal, 'B16/1' No 61411 (originally No 908) takes on water at Thornaby shed. The gantry type of water feed was installed as part of the modern facilities provided when the new shed designed to handle up to 200 steam locomotives,was opened in 1958. *Kevin Hughes*

Below:
The 'B16s' were seen on a variety of duties, not only on their native North Eastern, but elsewhere on the LNER system. Here we see No 931 very much on its home ground, passing Holgate Racecourse platform near York with its impressive battery of signals. The train is an up military special and the date is around 1933. *Real Photos (T6789)*

Left:
No 846 is taking the Church Fenton line at Chaloners Whin Junction with an up goods on 3 August 1936. The original wheel-and-handle smokebox door fastening has been replaced by the usual LNER double-handle type.
E. R. Morten

Below left:
'B16s' did not often find themselves in charge of titled expresses, but c1935 the up 'Scarborough Flyer' is commencing its journey in the care of No 845, Scarborough's mineral engine at the time, substituting for a 'D49' 4-4-0.
W. Oliver

Bottom left:
After World War 2, York 'B16s' were seen in the King's Cross area on occasion, generally in place of a rostered 'V2'. On 29 September 1946, No 1459 (originally No 1376) is working northwards near Ganwick with a fitted freight. Sometimes they were used on excursion trains to the capital; no fewer than five were seen in London on 10 August 1953.
H. C. Casserley

Above right:
After overhaul at York carriage works, one of the sets forming the non-stop 'Flying Scotsman' is being worked up to London by 'B16' No 844, on 2 June 1934. The train is seen passing through Grantham; the 'B16' would probably come off at New England. *T. G. Hepburn/ Rail Archive Stephenson*

Right:
A scene outside Sheffield Victoria station on 30 August 1958, not many years after electrification. The empty stock of a train from York is being drawn into Nunnery carriage sidings, with 'B16/1' No 61412 (originally No 909), which had brought the train in, assisting in the rear. Note the Thompson three-compartment Brake Third next to the engine.
K. R. Pirt

61412

Left:
On the Great Central, near Tibshelf, No 61458 (originally No 1375) is rolling downhill towards Nottingham with an up freight on 29 September 1959.
M. Mensing

Below:
One of the first 'B16s' to be built, and on 27 August 1960 within months of the end of its 40-year life, No 61478 (originally No 849) is passing Londesborough Road on its way to Scarborough Central with a relief train from York.
J. Cupit

61478

Left:
Now classed 'B16/1', No 61423, passes Burton Lane, York, with the 9.10am York-Scarborough train on 12 August 1961. The engine was withdrawn in the following month, and this is believed to have been the last occasion but one on which a 'B16' was used on passenger work.
P. J Lynch

Below:
For many years an empty coaching stock train left Newcastle at 9.20am for Holloway carriage sidings, where it was due at 12.50am the following morning. The load was such that the train was almost invariably double-headed. 'B16/1' No 61458 (originally No 1375, built in 1923) and 'V2' No 60949 (originally No 3651, built in 1942) are in charge, passing Stockton; the date is uncertain, but probably in the mid-1950s. *Ian Allan Library*

Left:
York was the postwar home of many 'B16s' and one of its allocation at the time, No 61460, is seen entering Doncaster from the north with a freight train on 31 August 1954. *Brian Morrison*

Above:
Passing Chaloners Whin signalbox, 'B16/2' No 1435 is following the Leeds road with a train from Edinburgh in 1948. This engine was the first of the class to be rebuilt by Gresley, in June 1937, and, in July 1964, the last to be withdrawn. It lasted almost as long in its Gresley form as in Raven's original.
Real Photos (23676)

Below:
No 922 was the first 'B16' to be rebuilt to 'B16/3' by Edward Thompson, in April 1944. Practically all the class were stationed at York in the late 1940s, and No 922 — evidently recently out of shops, judging by its external condition is seen passing through Nottingham Victoria with a Woodford-Annesley train of coal empties. *T. G. Hepburn/ Rail Archive Stephenson*

Facing page, top:
Steam and diesel traction at Hull Paragon, 1963. On Saturday 17 August, Thompson 'B16/3' No 61472 is hauling the 11.10am to Edinburgh, whilst English Electric Type 3 diesel-electric No D6734 leaves with the Hull portion of the 'Yorkshire Pullman'. The two trains will run on parallel tracks to West Parade Junction, the Edinburgh train turning north to Cottingham and York, the Pullman west towards Hessle and Doncaster. *Peter Brumby*

Facing page, bottom:
Good front-end detail can be seen in this close-up of 'B16/3' No 61461, one of a few of the class sent in their final years to the ex-Lancashire & Yorkshire shed at Mirfield, between Huddersfield and Dewsbury. The engine was photographed on 26 March 1963, only months before withdrawal. *John K. Morton*

Above left:
'B16/3' No 61417, rebuilt in 1945 when No 921, is seen at Northallerton, heading a down partly-fitted goods train on the fast line past a 'D20' 4-4-0 travelling northwards light engine. *Ian Allan Library*

Left:
A fitted freight for Whitemoor is seen at Gainsborough Trent Junction, c1955, headed by 'B16/3' No 61434 which appears to have a defective smokebox door fastening. Built at Darlington in 1922 and converted to Thompson's specification in 1949, this engine was originally No 2363. *Trevor Pinyoun/ Gresley Society Collection*

This picture:
In later years 'B16s' were often seen on the Great Central — almost always on fitted freight. Left-hand drive 'B16/3' No 61417 is travelling southwards past Belgrave and Birstall on 24 July 1961. The engine appears to be in good condition, working well, with a wisp of steam at the safety valves. *M. Mitchell*

3

Great Central 4-6-0s

Ninety 4-6-0s of Great Central origin came into LNER stock at the Grouping, and a further 10 were added in 1923-24 to make 100 in all. They were in nine different classes, with three different cylinder configurations and six diameters of driving wheel; the smallest class numerically consisted of two and the largest 38. They were used on a variety of duties on the Great Central system, but could also be seen regularly at York, and after the Grouping were visitors to King's Cross. In considering this assortment of locomotives it is also necessary to have regard to other contemporary Great Central classes, as the development of 4-4-0 and 4-4-2 locomotives on that railway is closely associated with that of the 4-6-0s; all were products of that renowned locomotive engineer, John G. Robinson.

Robinson received his early training at Swindon, and left the Great Western to join the Waterford & Limerick Railway in Ireland, soon being promoted to take responsibility for the rolling stock. During the 12 years in which he was in charge he built 33 new locomotives in a dozen different classes, none of which was of any significant note; the largest were three 4-4-0s of very modest dimensions. Meanwhile, towards the end of the 19th century the Manchester, Sheffield & Lincolnshire Railway changed its title to the Great Central Railway, and opened its London Extension from Annesley to Marylebone. Shortly afterwards steps were taken to appoint a new Locomotive Superintendent to replace Harry Pollitt who, it appears, resigned after differences with his Board over the performance of his Department; Robinson was given the appointment in 1900, becoming Chief Mechanical Engineer in 1902.

Robinson found that the best locomotives available for express passenger work were a series of 4-4-0s originating in a design by Thomas Parker, Pollitt's predecessor, and which had been developed by Pollitt into a class of 33, possessing 7ft driving wheels and 14,421lb tractive effort. Also, some 4-2-2s were in course of delivery, these being intended to work the fast but light trains on the London Extension. Robinson's initial assessment of the locomotive situation was that more powerful engines were needed all round, and to deal with passenger work he introduced a 4-4-0 which was significantly in advance of Pollitt's last design (and much more so than his own for the Waterford & Limerick). However, this was no more than a first step on the way to still larger engines, and it is clear that even in his early years in office he was determined to make his mark as a locomotive engineer.

One of Robinson's contemporaries at Swindon had been G. J. Churchward, who succeeded William Dean as Chief Mechanical Engineer in June 1902, and remained with the Great Western for the whole of his career. Towards the end of his period in office, Dean had been responsible for a number of experimental locomotives aimed at establishing the criteria for a standard range of classes which would meet the needs of the GWR in accordance with the most up-to-date practice. Churchward was influential in this work, one result of which was the appearance in March 1902 of the unique No 100, the first of the Great Western line of large wheel 4-6-0s. In the November of the same year Robinson also brought out his first 4-6-0, thus making a significant move forward from medium sized 4-4-0s in little more than two years since taking up his office. The Great Western engine had benefited from several years of experimentation, and of course Churchward had all the resources of Swindon behind him, whereas Robinson had only limited experience plus that of the design office and workshops at Gorton to support him. It is possible however that Beyer Peacock, with all their familiarity with large locomotives built for export, were glad to be able to lend him assistance, as there had been close collaboration between the railway and the manufacturers for many years. However, his new 4-6-0 was not intended for front line passenger work, but to meet a specific locomotive need — namely, to deal with the increasingly important North Sea fish traffic. One important difference between the Great Central and Great Western classes lay in the design of the valves. Unlike the conventional (for the time) slide valves of the Robinson engines, Churchward made use of long-lap, long-travel piston valves, but this was not disclosed in information published at the time, and this feature, and the benefits flowing from it, remained a Swindon secret for many years.

So, Robinson's first 4-6-0 was a straightforward design with 6ft driving wheels, primarily intended to deal with the through trains carrying fish landed at Grimsby and moved by the Great Central to London, Manchester and several other destinations, including traffic passing to the Great Western via the Banbury spur; a succession of fish trains left Grimsby between 5pm and 9pm on weekday evenings. These new locomotives were referred to officially as Class 8, and unofficially as the 'Fish Engines', a soubriquet which followed them throughout their lives, although their work in later years took them to other duties. Incidentally, it should be noted that fish traffic on the Great Central was conveyed by fast trains which were comparable in weight with many contemporary passenger trains; moreover, a number of bogie fish vans had been built to take part in this traffic, and often a passenger train would have a number of fish vans attached at the rear.

There had been a shortage of engines on the Great Central for some years — this was a factor in Pollitt's resignation — and Robinson was required to improve matters. Before he took up his office, a number of engines — about 40 — had been hired from other railways to help out, and it was a point in his favour that he was able to arrange their return in batches so that all had gone back by March 1902.

The new 4-6-0s were first referred to officially in December 1901, when it was decided that they were to be the subject of outside tender, as Gorton Works were being extended at the time, and were heavily engaged in reducing a backlog of repairs, as well as producing urgently needed 0-6-0s. The reference in the

Above:
One of the first batch of 'Fish' engines, 'B5' No 6070 still retained much of its original appearance until it was rebuilt in May 1936 with a superheated boiler of larger diameter. It is seen shortly before then near Littlefield Crossing, Grimsby, with the 11.49am from New Holland to Cleethorpes. The short journey and the vintage MSL stock belie the 'express' headcode. *E. R. Morten*

Left:
Rebuilt with a superheated boiler similar to that fitted to the 'Q4' 0-8-0s, 'B5' No 5183 is leaving for the south c1935 with the York section of the 'North Country Continental'. The through portion has been strengthened by four elderly Great Northern non-corridor coaches, the first pair of which can be seen to be articulated on the Gresley principle.
LPC/Ian Allan Library (6966)

GCR Locomotive Committee minutes mentions 'Six wheels coupled tender engines with leading bogie for working Grimsby and London fish trains, express goods and heavy excursion traffic'. Tenders were received from six manufacturers, Beyer Peacock's being the highest at £4,055 per engine, and Neilson Reid (soon to become part of the North British Locomotive Company) the lowest at £3,720. It was recommended that the order should go to Beyer Peacock if they could get down to Neilson's figure, but this they were evidently unable to do, as Neilson got the order at a reduced price of £3,700. All six appeared before the end of 1902, and were given the Nos 1067 to 1072.

Undoubtedly Robinson had taken note of the NER 'S' class, as, apart from the cylinder diameter, the dimensions were virtually the same — even down to the wheel spacing — the only significant difference in design being the use in the GCR class of the Belpaire firebox. In this Robinson was influenced by Swindon practice, although Pollitt had already introduced this refinement in his later engines and Robinson continued to make use of it. However, as discussed in Chapter 6, the predominantly hard water supplied to the GCR engines was later believed to have a greater adverse effect upon Belpaire boilers than on round-topped ones. Perhaps the grate was a little better than that of the 'S', and undoubtedly the smaller cylinders gave an improved boiler/cylinder relationship, as the Class 8s do not appear to have given rise to the criticism of lack of steam which followed the introduction of the first NER 4-6-0s. However, this may be attributed in part to the different duties to which the engines were first put: Robinson did not intend his to take over the best passenger services, and on the fast fish workings for

'B5' No 6068, heads northwards from Peterborough c1927 with an excursion train consisting mainly of a Great Northern close-coupled suburban set. *L&GRP, courtesy David & Charles (16319)*

which they were built, they performed competently and were a considerable improvement on the 0-6-0s which otherwise would have been employed.

Not only were the two classes of 4-6-0 similar in mechanical aspects, but they were alike in appearance, with outside cylinders driving on to the centre pair of coupled wheels, inside Stephenson's link motion, and large splashers. They differed of course in detail, the Robinson engines featuring the cutaway style of cab, contrasting with the double windows of the North Eastern version, as well as a slightly higher running plate, exposed safety valves and an elegant cast iron chimney. Both designs featured the wheel-and-handle type of smokebox door fastening. The GWR No 100 — of which neither Worsdell nor Robinson would have had knowledge before it appeared — was quite different in many aspects, although it did not, on its first appearance, have Churchward's characteristic tapered boiler.

Robinson's next consideration also followed GWR and NER experiments, as in seeking to develop a new class of locomotive for fast and heavy passenger work he looked carefully at the respective merits of the 4-4-2 and 4-6-0 types, and in 1903-04 built examples of each with identical boilers, cylinders and other components. Because of pressure on the Gorton drawing office, Beyer Peacock carried out the detailed design work to Robinson's specification and also built the first two of each type. The 4-4-2s were given the GCR classification '8B', and the 4-6-0s, '8C'; the LNER equivalents were 'C4' and 'B1' (later 'B18') respectively. The boiler and firebox were measurably larger than those of the earlier Class 8, and to enable the Atlantics to be converted to 4-6-0s if this were decided upon at a later date, the firebox of the 4-4-2 was shallower than it could have been, as this wheel arrangement permitted a deeper box than one restricted by the trailing coupled axle of the 4-6-0. Also, to afford a further comparison, one of each pair was provided with 19in diameter cylinders, and the others given cylinders ½in larger. Evidently the former were the more successful, as this dimension was applied to later batches of Atlantics as they were built. However, on the more fundamental choice between the 4-4-2 and the 4-6-0 types, Robinson soon came down in favour of the 4-4-2, at least for the time being, as another 27 '8Bs' were built, as well as, in another experiment, four Compound Atlantics. No further '8Cs' were turned out, the original pair remaining the only examples of their class, but conversely it was not felt worthwhile to convert them to 4-4-2s, although this could have been done without a great deal of expense. One potential advantage of the Atlantic wheel arrangement, the capability to provide a deeper firebox, was adopted in the later examples to be built, and the two originals were provided with this refinement when replacement boilers were acquired.

It is of interest to compare the Robinson attitude towards the choice of Atlantic or 4-6-0 with that of Churchward and Worsdell. The latter did not build equivalent locomotives of each type, evidently deciding on the Atlantic for passenger work from his experience with the 'S' and 'S1' classes, but Churchward, in the same way as Robinson, built like-for-like examples of both — indeed, not only with two but with four cylinders. Moreover, Churchward went further, when, having finally decided that his preference lay with six-coupled engines, he converted his Atlantics to 4-6-0s. Like Robinson and Worsdell, Churchward also experimented with compounding, but purchased three Compound Atlantics from France instead of building his own. These showed that no significant advantage was to be gained from a compound arrangement, but they nevertheless remained in their original form until withdrawal.

Churchward's decision to discard the Atlantic type was part of an overall policy of concentration wherever possible on six- or eight-coupled locomotives, except for certain lighter duties. A major advantage of the 4-6-0 over the 4-4-2 was of course the greater surefootedness given by the extra adhesion of the six-coupled wheelbase, which on the other hand had to be weighed against the opportunity for better firebox design offered by the Atlantic. Great Western and Great Central locomotive tasks were by no means similar; the GWR possessed a generally more level main line between London and Exeter, but beyond were the severe South Devon banks. However, it may be considered that the profiles of the line to Birmingham and Chester, and the West to North route from Maindee to Shrewsbury, were not greatly dissimilar to the main lines of the Great Central. Great Western loads were generally heavier, and one can only conclude that the final choice between 4-4-2 and 4-6-0 lay in individual preference, possibly influenced by lingering doubts on the part of Atlantic protagonists that six-coupled wheels were a hindrance to speed.

Despite his final preference for the 4-6-0 type, Churchward did not at that time introduce a smaller wheeled 4-6-0 specifically for fast goods work, although one was included in proposals drawn up in 1901 for a standard range of locomotives. When a mixed traffic design larger than a 0-6-0 was eventually introduced, in 1911, it was not a 4-6-0 but a 2-6-0; a 6ft variant of the 'Saint' class had to wait until 1924 when Churchward's successor, C. B. Collett, converted *Saint Martin* into a mixed traffic locomotive with 6ft wheels, as the predecessor of the well known 'Hall' class. A 5ft 8in version did not materialise until 1936, when Collett introduced the 'Grange' class as a replacement for the 1911 Mogul.

Robinson's third essay with 4-6-0s was a class of 10, classified '8F' by the GCR, and 'B4' by the LNER, which were virtual repeats of the '8Cs' but with a driving wheel diameter slightly reduced to 6ft 6in. They were all delivered by Beyer Peacock in 1906 and put to work on the fish trains from Grimsby; they were more powerful than the original Class 8, and their larger wheels gave them a better turn of speed. Some were stationed at Neasden and, as might be expected, were frequently used on passenger work, although there was never any suggestion that they might oust the Atlantics from their position as the first choice locomotives on the London extension. The '8Fs' were numbered 1095 to 1104, No 1097 being named *Immingham*, after having worked the special train carrying invited personages to the ceremony of cutting the first sod at the new dock at Immingham, on 12 July 1906. As a result, the members of the class were unofficially dubbed the 'Imminghams'.

The '8Fs' were followed by a batch of 10 similar 4-6-0s, classified '8G' (LNER 'B9'), but with coupled wheels having the unusual diameter of 5ft 3in; they had the same boiler as the '8Bs' and '8Fs', but the smaller firebox as fitted to the original Class 8. These too were built by Beyer Peacock, but the maker's internal order number and works numbers point to an original intention to construct them before the '8Fs'; however, they followed the latter in the locomotive register by taking Nos 1109 to 1114. These small-wheeled 4-6-0s were used at first on fast goods trains from Manchester over the Pennines to Sheffield, and on to Lincoln and Grimsby, but they were later replaced on these duties, and spent part of their LNER life on Cheshire Lines services, after which their principal use was on Deansgate to Colwick jobs.

It is convenient at this point to consider the policy which was evolving in Robinson's mind towards the future provision of express passenger locomotives at the end of the first decade of the 20th century. By 1906, 31 Atlantics had been built, including the four Compounds, and these had settled down on the haulage of the best Great Central trains between Marylebone and Manchester, with support provided by the 4-4-0s, 40 of which had been built by 1904. The four classes of 4-6-0 were mainly employed on fast goods services, helping out on passenger work as occasion demanded, but additional locomotives were now needed to replace older engines.

At this time it is possible that Robinson was impressed by the Caledonian 4-6-0 No 903 *Cardean*, which was enjoying a high reputation at the time, as, instead of a new 4-4-0, a 4-6-0 with 6ft 9in driving wheels and inside cylinders emerged from Gorton in December 1912. This was evidently intended to take over the hardest work from the Atlantics, as the design showed a further increase in dimensions over the '8B' and '8C' classes; moreover this was the first GCR express engine to be provided with a superheater from new. The grate area remained at 26sq ft, but the heating surface went up to 2,817sq ft in a boiler of 5ft 6in diameter, and the cylinders to 21½in diameter. They were fine-looking locomotives, an important visual feature being the continuous splasher covering much of the coupled wheels. They were evidently considered to be the commencement of a new style of external design, as well as a source of considerable pride to their designer, as they were given the class number 1 (later, LNER 'B2' class). The first one was named *Sir Sam Fay*, after the Great Central General Manager, who had received a knighthood earlier in the year when King George V opened Immingham Dock, and five more of the class were given the names of cities served by the Great Central system. All came from Gorton, the first five between December 1912 and March 1913, the last not until December of that year; they received running Nos 423 to 428. In later LNER days the classification was altered to 'B19' when, in 1945, Edward Thompson commenced the reconstruction of Gresley's 'B17s', these rebuilds assuming the 'B2' classification.

However, the Class 1 was disappointing in service. The ashpan design was less than satisfactory, restricting the supply of air through the grate, and consequently trouble was sometimes experienced in getting the large boiler to steam adequately. This difficulty was exacerbated by the cramped arrangements of the piston valves and of the superheater, although it is fair to say that in the early days of superheating, design offices were still experimenting with the dimensions of this newly popularised device. Further problems arose with the driving axleboxes, which were subjected to hard pounding from the large cylinders, this in turn leading on occasion to overheating. (This was a problem which beset all designers of large, inside-cylinder locomotives, due to restrictions imposed on the axlebox layout.)

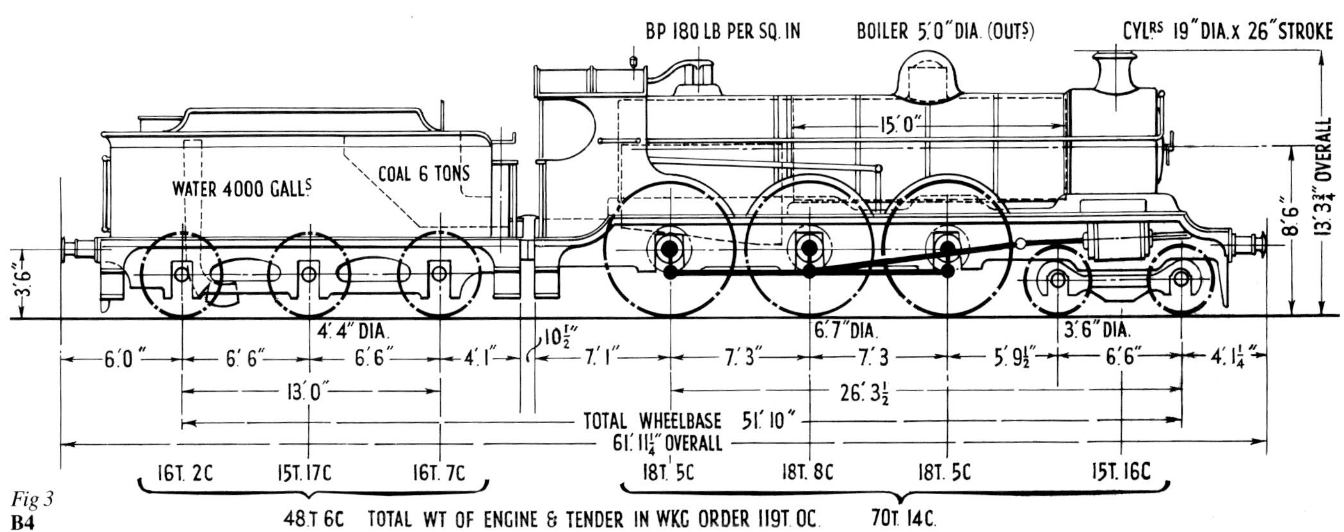

Fig 3
B4

A 4-4-0 design which was being developed at the same time as that of the 4-6-0 appeared in 1913, and followed the Class 1 in running number order as Nos 429 to 438. Classified '11E', they were evidently intended to complement the contemporary 4-6-0s, being given similar lines, notably the single overall splashers. Their dimensions were larger than those of Robinson's earlier 4-4-0s, but less than those of the 'Sir Sam Fays'. The boiler was 5ft 3in in diameter, with a total heating surface of 1,963sq ft, and since the firegrate was the same as that of the 4-6-0s, but the cylinders were reduced in diameter to 20in, the locomotives were better proportioned. Consequently, although the nominal tractive effort was less, they steamed better and hence, in comparable circumstances, were capable of developing more power at the drawbar than the 4-6-0s. So, instead of performing a supporting role, the '11Es' took over the main burden of the Marylebone services, although they by no means replaced the Atlantics entirely.

A third class constructed in the same period, with many similar characteristics, was a further 4-6-0 with the same firebox and boiler as the Class 1, but with 5ft 7in driving wheels. These were the '1A' class (LNER 'B8' class) and were known as the 'Glenalmonds' as the first was given the name of the Scottish seat of the Chairman, Sir Alexander Henderson. This was numbered 4 in the GCR register, but the next eight continued the sequence begun by *Sir Sam Fay*, receiving Nos 439 to 446. In all, 11 were built, the last emerging from Gorton in January 1915. The 'Glenalmonds' were generally confined to freight working, with some assistance on excursion trains at weekends. Their smaller driving wheels gave them a somewhat squat appearance, emphasised by the straight lines of the running plate, which was not raised to match that of the 'Sir Sam Fays'.

It is not entirely certain that these three inside-cylindered classes all formed a single concept — first and second rank express passenger, and mixed traffic — but their production at Gorton certainly overlapped. One school of thought considers that the shortcomings of the Class 1 were soon apparent, and in consequence Robinson reverted to a 4-4-0 design, which was hastily worked up in the drawing office and put in hand at Gorton works, even before the batch of Class 1s had been completed. As events turned out, the '11Es' were amongst the most successful inside-cylinder 4-4-0s ever to have been built in Britain. Since the first examples were named after members of the Board of the Great Central Railway, they became known as the 'Directors', and after improvements in detail 11 more were built, together with a further 24 to LNER order for service in Scotland after the Grouping.

The following table gives the order of completion at Gorton of the three classes:

Class	*Nos*	*Completed*
1	423-427	December 1912 to March 1913
1A	4	June 1913
11E	429-438	August to December 1913
1	428	December 1913
1A	439-446, 279, 280	July 1914 to January 1915

(NB: '8K' class 2-8-0s were also being built during this period, 26 being turned out between April 1913 and June 1914.)

It would appear probable however that the three classes were conceived as complementary, with the 4-4-0s in a supporting role, but soon after they had entered service the '11Es' were found to be the more successful on fast passenger work, and consequently took over the brunt of this. Perhaps it was the reason for the protracted delay to the completion of No 428.

Robinson's 2-8-0 was by far the most widely known of his designs, if not of all British locomotive classes. It was adopted by the War Department as a standard locomotive for use in the service of the armed forces abroad, and to give employment after World War 1; no fewer than 666 were built in all, 521 to Government order in 1917-19. In 1918 Robinson enlarged the design, providing a boiler 5ft 6in in diameter, and at the same

Right:
A nice study of Sheffield Victoria in 1939; 'B5' No 5183 is probably one of the two standing pilots. As well as being engaged in shunting operations, these engines had to be prepared to take over in the event of a main line failure. Note the elevated position of the station, and the partial replacement of GCR signals by LNER upper quadrants.
Hughes Junction

Far right:
One of the pair of 4-6-0s built for comparison with the similarly dimensioned Atlantics, No 5195 is seen at Woodford shed in 1937 — its main duties at the time being the haulage of fish trains. Rigid application of the LNER policy of restricting green livery to a small number of selected classes led to these two 'B1s' being painted green, whilst the 'Directors' and Atlantics working main line passenger services were black. The 4-6-0s were said to 'keep their feet better' than the equivalent 4-4-2s. *Crown Copyright/ National Railway Museum Collection (PRW 1656)*

time a 4-6-0 was built with the same boiler and cylinders, but with 5ft 8in driving wheels, to create a mixed traffic equivalent of the 2-8-0. The shallow, elongated splasher was similar, the running plate being raised on the 4-6-0 to allow for the larger diameter driving wheels. Only one was constructed initially, concurrently with the enlarged 2-8-0s, and was classified '8N', later to be known as the 'B6' under the LNER. It was reported to steam well, and to give fewer complaints of overheating than the '1As'. The reasons were first, that whilst the boiler was of the same 5ft 6in diameter as that of the 'Sir Sam Fays' it was 2ft 3in shorter, and the tube arrangements were different, giving the fireman a better opportunity to maintain steam pressure. Secondly, the reversion to outside cylinders allowed the provision of adequate bearings for the coupled wheels. Nevertheless, despite the evident advantages of this new design, it was two years before any others appeared, and these were only two in number, being turned out from Gorton in 1922. The reason for this was another change in conception by Robinson of how best to obtain good performance from a 4-6-0.

Whilst the '8N' represented the continuation of a series of locomotives of different wheel arrangements, but all with two outside cylinders, even before the first of the class was built a completely new passenger 4-6-0 had been specified. This was to be '9P' (LNER 'B3') and whilst employing the Class 1 firebox and boiler, these were allied to four 16in×26in cylinders, giving a nominal tractive effort of 25,415lb, 10% greater than that of the Class 1s, and making the '9Ps' the most powerful express passenger locomotives on the LNER at Grouping, apart from the Great Northern and North Eastern Pacifics. The four cylinders were mounted in line, but the drive was divided, and to

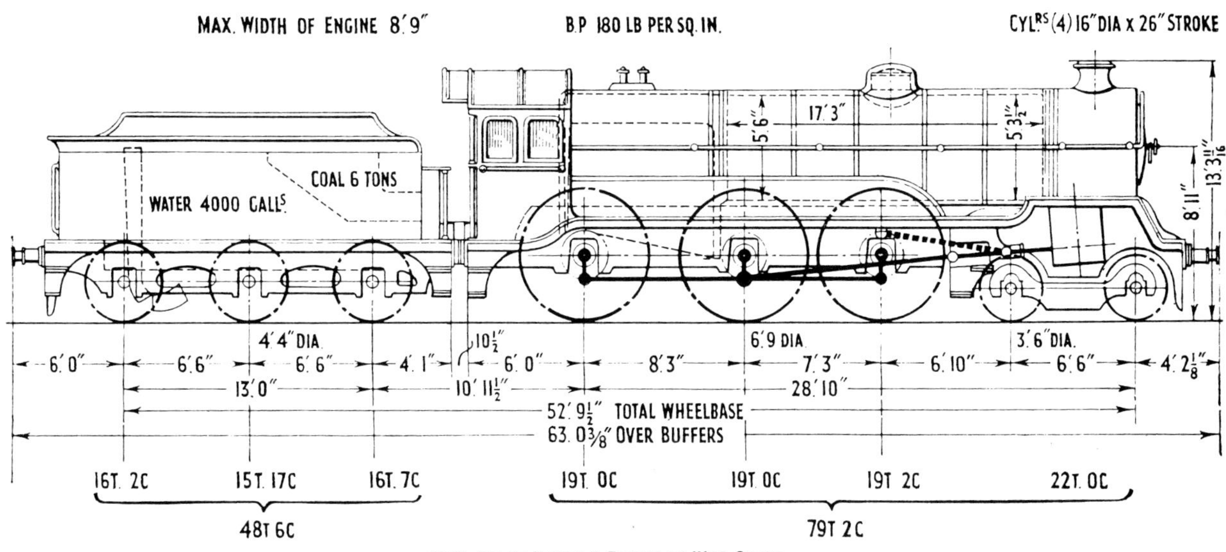

Fig 4
B3/1

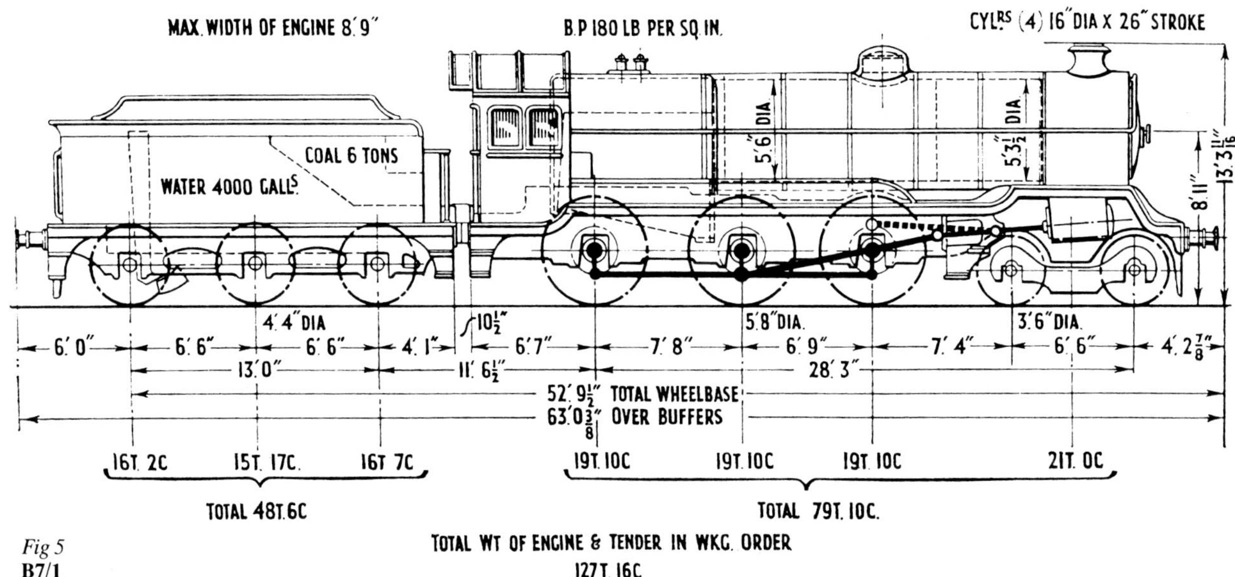

Fig 5
B7/1

avoid an overlong connecting rod the outside slidebars were set well back, resulting in elongated piston rods. Two sets of Stephenson's link motion were installed between the frames, the drive for the piston valves of the outside cylinders being derived from that of the inside valves. The positioning of the cylinders led to the running plate being raised above them, and this, together with a massive motion bracket, tended to detract from the appearance of the locomotive, particularly in comparison with the simplicity of outline of the Class 1. The first of the '9Ps', No 1169, was in fact completed at Gorton eight months before the first '8N', and was given the name of the Great Central Chairman, now Lord Faringdon, who later became the Deputy Chairman of the LNER; no more were built until 1920, when a batch of five was turned out. However, although they were said to be an improvement on the 'Sir Sam Fays', a lot was left to be desired, especially from the points of view of good steaming and reasonable coal consumption. No 1165 received the name *Valour* in commemoration of the sacrifice of Great Central employees who gave their lives in the Great War. One of the nameplates is preserved at the National Railway Museum at York. The other was placed in St Barnabas Church, Openshaw, but sadly it was stolen some years ago.

It is not easy to grasp how Robinson managed to obtain authority to build what was so obviously an express passenger engine in the middle of the Great War, when normally only locomotives intended mainly for freight haulage would have been sanctioned. It had, in fact, been developed in secret, and when eventually brought to the knowledge of the GCR Locomotive Committee in November 1917 — the same month in which it left Gorton — it was described as a 'four-cylinder mixed train engine' (*sic*) and something of an experiment. It had been built during the previous couple of years as opportunity permitted, using spare material and duplicate parts — and this was in a period when Robinson regularly reported to the Committee on the difficulties of obtaining materials needed for locomotive repairs! The later batch of five were clearly referred to as 'mixed traffic engines', but there is no evidence that they were ever used regularly on goods trains. On the other hand, the need for larger engines was made clear when, due to the divergence of much of the Manchester traffic from the Midland to the Great Central during World War 1, double heading had to be resorted to on occasion.

Although the '9Ps' were used initially on the services between Marylebone and Manchester, reduced postwar loadings demonstrated that these trains could still be more competently handled by the 'Directors' and Atlantics, 11 more of the 4-4-0s having been built between 1919 and 1922, with minor improvements to the design. Consequently, when the Great Central was merged with the Great Eastern and Great Northern into the Southern Area of the LNER after the Grouping, the opportunity offered itself for the class, now given the classification 'B3', to operate outside the GCR system. W. G. P. Maclure had been the Locomotive Running Superintendent of the Great Central, and after the formation of the LNER he was promoted to a similar position for the whole of the Southern Area. Consequently, when in the summer of 1923 a Pullman Car service was introduced between King's Cross, Harrogate and Newcastle, Maclure considered that the 'B3s' would be suitable for the haulage of these trains between King's Cross and Leeds, and by the following year all six were allocated to this work, being stationed at King's Cross and Copley Hill sheds. However, they were not altogether made welcome on the Great Northern section, as they required a more careful method of firing than the Atlantics to which the crews were accustomed; nevertheless they enjoyed a period of four years on the Pullman turns, but all had returned to Gorton by 1927. Maclure persisted with his efforts to employ a Great Central class on the Great Northern, and a small number of 'Director' class 4-4-0s were sent to Copley Hill, where they worked turn and turn about with Ivatt Atlantics on the fast Pullman services. As on the GCR main line, the 'Directors' proved more successful than the 'B3s', but all had returned to their parent location by 1933.

Despite the evident success of the three '8N' mixed traffic 4-6-0s, Robinson decided that to meet the increasing need for this kind of locomotive, a more powerful design was required, and that four cylinders would be desirable. Believing that the shorter boiler of the '8Ns' would be inadequate, he applied the boiler and cylinders of the 'Lord Faringdon' class to what was to be his last design, a general purpose locomotive with 5ft 8in driving wheels, of which the tractive effort was a respectable 29,952lb. These engines were urgently needed, and 28 were constructed in little over a year, between May 1921 and August 1922. Pressure for delivery was such that only 13 were built at Gorton, the remainder being contracted to the Vulcan Foundry (10) and Beyer Peacock (five). Another 10 were included in the initial LNER building programme, the last coming from Gorton in March 1924. Following closely the 6ft 8in '9P' 4-6-0s, they were given the Great Central classification '9Q', but were better

Right:
The similarity between the 'B1s' and the 'C4s' can be seen in this postwar scene of 4-4-2 No 2908 (GCR No 1084) climbing the 1 in 105 from Rickmansworth to Chorley Wood with a down stopping train. *H. C. Casserley*

Below:
No 6097 *Immingham* is seen on the turntable at Grantham shed in 1931, nicely turned out in lined green, having worked in on a train from Leeds. Note the similarities with the 'B1s', 'B5s' and 'C4s'. The tall, plain tapered chimney would have made the engine too high to come within the LNER composite load gauge. *Crown Copyright/National Railway Museum Collection (ACC/LNE 301)*

known on the LNER as the 'B7s'. In preliminary Boardroom discussions they were referred to as 'four-cylinder Genalmonds', and it has been said that they were known in some quarters as 'Black Pigs' because of their propensity for high coal consumption, but there is no conclusive evidence that they were any worse in this respect than many other contemporary designs.

Robinson's last 4-6-0 design was comparable in tractive effort with the NER 'S3', although it differed in many important features, being provided with four cylinders instead of three, and a Belpaire instead of a round-topped boiler. Total heating surface, including superheater, was greater by some 22%, the boiler being packed with larger diameter tubes; however, this did not necessarily mean that the 'B7' could steam better, as water circulation could have been impeded by the additional volume of pipework. The final 10 'B7s', completed under LNER auspices, carried cabs and boiler mountings of reduced height, so that their sphere of operation was enlarged, whilst four of the batch were provided with larger steam chests, somewhat altering their front end appearance.

A number of advances in detail design appeared as the sequence of GCR 4-6-0s evolved. Superheating was first introduced on Classes 1 and 1A, which also received piston valves when new, and there was a general enlargement of dimensions. Another item of note was the introduction of a more commodious side window cab in place of the cutaway pattern, as first seen on No 1165 in 1920. After Grouping a number of major and minor improvements took place in the older classes, notably the replacement of boilers using saturated steam by ones with superheaters. This did not necessarily improve the appearance of the engines concerned, as it resulted in a higher pitched boiler; when the mountings of certain classes were cut down to conform to the group loading-gauge, the earlier proportions were lost. However, the detail change which displeased many observers was the replacement of the gracefully curved Robinson chimney by an LNER version known as the 'flowerpot'. The original was no doubt expensive and prone to cracking, and replacements were necessary, but it was widely held that these could have been produced with greater sensitivity to the engine's appearance. This was eventually accepted by the CME's Department, as after some years a design more akin to the original was introduced. Even so, appreciation of chimney styles is very much a matter of individual preference, and there are those who in some cases prefer the more functional 'flowerpot' — designed, it is said, to provide the most efficient ejection of exhaust gases. Possibly a consensus could be reached by accepting that the sweeping curves of the earlier Robinson designs were nicely complemented by the contours of their original chimney, whilst the 'flowerpot' was well suited to the 'B7s'. A further modification was seen when header discharge valves were placed at the side of the smokebox on some engines, but later the Gresley pattern was fitted in a less conspicuous position behind the chimney. Finally, a few 4-6-0s were converted to oil firing during periods of coal shortage in the early 1920s; in such cases, a rectangular oil tank was fitted in the tender.

The GCR 4-6-0s collectively earned a reputation of being heavy on coal, the two four-cylinder classes possibly even more so than the others, but on such evidence as is available they were little worse than many of their contemporaries on the LNER and elsewhere. (See Appendix IV for details of LNER 4-6-0s.) Nevertheless Gresley, prompted no doubt by operators who saw the 'B3s' as 'collier's friends', and wishing to emulate the LMS in experimenting with Caprotti poppet valves, sought authority to convert four of the class to the use of this type of valve. (He was at the same time fitting Lentz poppet valves to 'D49' 4-4-0s and 'B12' 4-6-0s.) However, the LNER Board baulked at the estimated price of £7,000, and only sanctioned two. These, Nos 6166/68, were duly modified in 1929, the gear being manufactured by Beardmore, under licence from the Italian designers. Coal consumption was reported to be reduced, but at the expense of mechanical reliability; the valve springs frequently fractured, as did the cast iron scrolls which operated the cams. A further source of difficulty lay in overheating of the cams, due to their being contained in an airtight box. After unsuccessful palliative action, the cam box cover was removed, but this in turn led to the ingress of grit, so that finally a modified cover was devised. However, the Caprotti-fitted engines did not spend an excess of time in the shops, the average annual mileage in 1931-34 amounting to 49,120 compared to 43,207 for the piston-valved engines — a 14% increase.

Careful records were kept between 1931 and 1934 of the overall coal consumption of the two conversions in comparison with the remainder of the class, as a result of which it was found that the Caprotti engines possessed a 19% advantage over those remaining unconverted. Gresley, evidently impressed, ordered specific comparative trials between Nos 6166 (Caprotti) and 6169 (piston valves). These took place on six occasions in 1935-36, the two locomotives hauling the 8.45am from Marylebone to Manchester, returning on the 2.20pm up, with a seven-coach train weighing some 240 tons gross. The piston-valved engine used 51.8lb of coal per mile (0.260lb/ton mile), the Caprotti only 40.8lb (0.203lb/ton mile), a saving of 21%. Both were free from mechanical defect during the period of the trials, and to add to its evident greater efficiency, No 6166 was reported to have gained on a sharply timed schedule.

Following these results, authority was given for another two to be converted, and Nos 6164 and 6167 were selected, the work being carried out in 1938. The system employed (which was a British design, manufactured by Armstrong Whitworth) was different in that steam, instead of springs, was applied to return the valves to their seats. The performance of the two engines was reported to be an even greater improvement on that of those retaining piston valves, and plans were in hand to convert these, as well as the 'B7' mixed traffic class, when the war intervened. The Caprotti-fitted engines were at first confined to Marylebone-Leicester workings, such as the night mails and the 2.32am down newspaper train, probably the hardest working on the London Extension; fitters acquainted with the special mechanism were not then available at every depot.

A much more radical conversion of a 'B3' was undertaken by Edward Thompson in 1943; indeed the locomotive appearing in the guise of No 6166 was almost a complete replacement, little more than the wheel centres and part of the frames remaining of the original locomotive. Thompson also gave thought to a reconstruction of the 'B7s', but this came to nothing. These two projects are discussed in Chapter 6.

Detailed accounts of GCR 4-6-0s in action are not easy to come by, except for the periods when they worked regularly on the Marylebone services. However, those records which do exist demonstrate that, like many locomotive classes, they were capable of good performances, when in first class condition and

No 6097 *Immingham* again, hauling a coal train near Dukeries Junction in 1947. The train would have originated in the Notts/Derby coalfield, and is probably destined for Immingham or New England.
P. Ransome-Wallis

Above:
Three of the 'B4s' were shedded at Lincoln in the late 1930s, where their main duty was to work the York portion of the 'North Country Continental' between York and Lincoln. This was quite a heavy train, although the schedule did not call for very fast running. No 6104 is seen heading the down train at Escrick in 1938. *Real Photos (23696)*

competently handled. Charles Rous-Marten was so impressed by No 195 that he declared 'it would be able to haul Marylebone station if it had been placed on wheels'. Its companion, No 196, was noted in 1905 as beating even time from Nottingham to Leicester, and carrying on in the same vein to Marylebone, the 103.1-mile journey taking only 103min. However, the load was no more than four bogies, with a gross weight of perhaps 120 tons, but this performance showed that the engine was capable of sustained high speeds, six-coupled wheels notwithstanding. The engine was said to have 'glided like a single wheeler, and to be capable of maintaining this speed with two or three times the load'. Four- or five-coach trains were the norm on the London Extension at this period, but the schedules were not easy. The main exit route from London was shared with the Metropolitan Railway, and was the subject of severe speed restrictions in places, notably at Rickmansworth. A time of 49min might be allowed for the 38 miles to Aylesbury, but from there to Leicester the running averaged almost a mile a minute, despite the long 1 in 176 banks. Nearly 30 years later, the same engine, by now LNER No 5196, deputised for a 'V2' on a Newcastle to Ashford troop train weighing 490 tons gross, and took 29¼min from Leicester to Rugby, averaging only 40mph over this 19.9-mile stretch, but achieving 70mph on the way.

Great Central 4-6-0s often worked regularly on the Great Northern main line, before as well as after the Grouping. GCR drivers were keen to show that their engines could match the Ivatt Atlantics, and No 196 is again recorded, this time running the 33.1 miles from Grantham to Retford, in 34min 40sec. In early post-Grouping days the 'Imminghams' were all allocated to Ardsley or Copley Hill sheds in Leeds, and regularly worked to Grantham or, on occasion, to King's Cross, on excursion trains. A number of records exist of such workings, notably of No 6096 hauling 465 gross tons between Wakefield and Doncaster, with a time of 22min 22sec for the 19.9 miles, including 3½ miles at 1 in 150. Beyond Doncaster, No 6095 with 450 tons took 20min 55sec to a stop at Retford (17.4 miles) and 38min 5sec on to Grantham, touching 70mph on the way. The 'Sir Sam Fays' also had a brief spell on the Great Northern main line, in fact being the first GCR class to be tried on the Pullman trains — the short-lived 'Sheffield Pullman' which ran via Retford and Nottingham being a regular working for this class. The reason given was that it was thought that their six-coupled wheels would enable the 'B2s' to handle the gradients between Nottingham and Sheffield better than the Ivatt Atlantics. Later, when stationed at Immingham, they supplemented the more usual 'B3s' and 'B7s' on the privately organised 'Eason's Special' excursion trains between Grimsby and King's Cross. A few Immingham men had first learned the road to King's Cross when working Navy leave specials.

Cecil J. Allen's recordings on the Great Central main line south of Sheffield almost always featured Atlantics or 'Directors'. Of the few 4-6-0s he travelled behind on this route, *Sir Sam Fay* himself, on a run in the last years before the Grouping, lost ¾min on the 26min schedule between Leicester and Nottingham, over a hilly road of 23.4 miles; the load was a six-coach train of 220 tons gross. Later, during the period when the trains were generally in the hands of the 'B17s', Caprotti-fitted No 6168 *Lord Stuart of Wortley* cut the 26min schedule by ¾min; LNER bogie stock had increased the weight of the train, six coaches now weighing 240 tons gross. A speed of 84mph was achieved at Ruddington.

No 6165 *Valour* is featured in a number of logs, in one of which, on an up Pullman in 1927, 85mph was reached on the descent of Stoke Bank, whilst with a wartime load of 565 tons from Wakefield to Grantham the engine, then just out of shops, was said to have performed as well as a 'V2' in moderate condition. The Caprotti-fitted 'B3s' were marginally faster than those with piston valves, 88mph having been recorded more than once at Whetstone. The smaller-wheeled 'B7s' seem to have been quite sprightly, and were in demand for hauling excursion traffic. Amongst good peformances recorded were 45mph at Helmdon, after 4½ miles up 1 in 176, with 385 tons, by No 5459 in 1936, and 77mph by No 5463 with the 2.32am down newspaper train at Gotham in 1930.

The great majority of Great Central engines were painted black, with red and white lining, but the prestige express engines were given a splendid livery of Brunswick green, lined out in black with white edging, red oxide underframes and polished brass beading. The four classes of large-wheeled 4-6-0s were seen in this state in their GCR days, except that three of the 'Sir Sam Fays' were painted black when first turned out from Gorton, and the 'B4s' were all in goods livery after their first shopping. However, they all assumed LNER green after the Grouping until this was replaced by unrelieved black in the wartime years. Even after the economy strictures of 1928, which

Similar in many respects to the 'Imminghams', the smaller-wheeled 'B9s' were also long-lived, all lasting 40 years or more. No 6111 is seen ex-works sometime in the 1930s, smartly turned-out with polished brass beading to the splashers. This engine was withdrawn for scrapping in 1939, but was overhauled instead and put back into service, eventually being the last of the class to go, in 1949. *Crown Copyright/National Railway Museum Collection (PRW 1101)*

Left:
In the mid-LNER period, 'B4s' were responsible for handling much of the traffic between Doncaster and Leeds. No 6098 was at Copley Hill shed for several years, and is seen at Doncaster in 1938 heading a connecting train with an East Coast express in the background. *Hughes Junction*

decreed that locomotives such as the GCR Atlantics and 'Directors' should be black, these 4-6-0 classes continued to be seen in green livery, which produced the anomaly of black engines hauling the best trains, whilst the green ones were generally on lesser duties.

Seventeen of the 100 Great Central 4-6-0s were given names, but three of the engines lost them in LNER days. One of these was 'B2' No 5427 *City of London*, whose name was removed in 1937 when one of the 'B17' class was streamlined to run the new 'East Anglian' train, and assumed the name. The others were No 6166 *Earl Haig*, after it had been rebuilt by Thompson, and No 6167 *Lloyd George*. This last instance arose when in the early summer of 1923 Queen Mary was travelling to Harrogate to stay with her daughter, Princess Mary, who lived nearby at Goldsborough Hall. No 6167 was rostered to take the train, but when the Chief General Manager saw the name on the engine he was horrified; not only was Lloyd George *persona non grata* with the railway authorities on account of his perceived advocacy of Nationalisation, but it was considered that Queen Mary would not have been pleased to learn that her train was in the hands of this particular politician. So, orders were sent to have the nameplates removed forthwith, but this was easier said than done since they formed an integral part of the beading which held the splashers together. In the event the nameplates were removed together with a foot of beading on each side, but they disappeared from sight until being discovered 40 years later when Top Shed was being demolished in 1963. It is doubtful whether Queen Mary was aware of the anxiety felt on her behalf.

In passing, it seems unjust that no locomotive was selected to commemorate the name of J. G. Robinson, who in addition to being amongst the most innovative of locomotive engineers (his superheater was widely used by Gresley) produced a long line of sturdy and generally competent engines. An officer was rarely accorded this honour in pre-Grouping days, but the Great Central Board agreed as far back as 1912 that their recently knighted General Manager should give his name to the first of a new class. However, No 1490 *Sir Sam Fay* was not followed by 'John G. Robinson' and when in early British Railways days some of the new Peppercorn Pacifics were given the names of locomotive engineers of the Great Northern and North Eastern Railways, it would have been appropriate for this eminent engineer to have been similarly commemorated.

In their last days, the LNER 1946 renumbering took the GCR 4-6-0s into the 1300 and 1400 series, but those surviving were given higher numbers to keep them clear of the advancing tide of Thompson 'B1' 4-6-0s, which took over most of the duties previously undertaken by Robinson's nine classes. Apart from 'B5' No 6070, scrapped in 1939, all survived World War 2, but were withdrawn in the early postwar years, the last being 'B4' No 6097 *Immingham* itself, in November 1950 — the only Great Central engine to receive postwar LNER green. Despite being the most useful of the classes, the 'B7s' were not kept in service any longer than the generality of Robinson's 4-6-0s, a few lasting only 23 years. The longest-lived of them all was one of the originals, 'B5' No 6069, with 46 years of honourable toil to its credit.

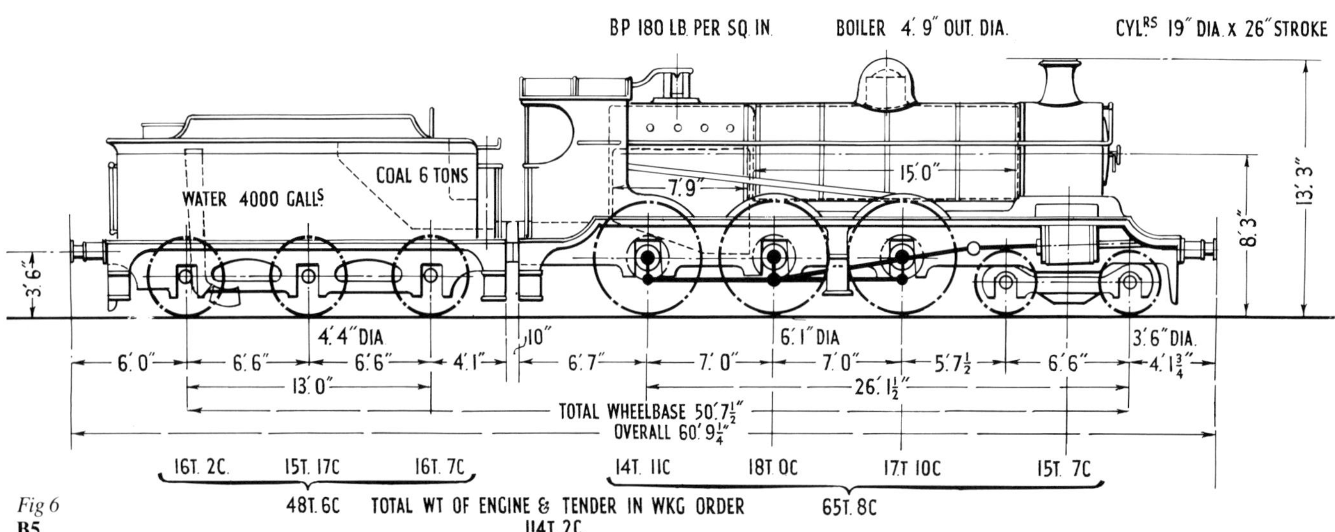

Fig 6
B5

Far left:
A 'B9' on passenger work in its early days. GCR No 1107 was photographed by W. Bradshaw in 1911 on a down express passing Abbey Lane sidings, Leicester. The tall chimney and the dome displayed by this engine gave all Robinson's older 4-6-0s an impressive appearance. Built by Beyer Peacock in Manchester in 1906, it had a lengthy life of almost 41 years. Note the re-railing jack by the smokebox.
Bucknall Collection/ Ian Allan Library

Top:
From 1934 to 1936 the three 'B6' 4-6-0s were shedded at Sheffield — first at Neepsend and later at the new depot at Darnall. They worked a variety of trains, but did not travel very far afield. No 5416 was the first to be built, in 1918, all three being withdrawn just before Nationalisation. *Hughes Junction*

Above left:
On what seems to have been a running-in turn after overhaul and repainting in early LNER livery, No 5416 is seen leaving Guide Bridge for Sheffield.
Real Photos (W4890)

Left:
No 5416 again, leaving York with an excursion to Scarborough. The period is the summer of 1929, soon after the engine had commenced a spell at Bradford. One of its drivers at this time was Ted Hailstone, who was later to gain renown as a top-link driver at King's Cross.
Real Photos (20679)

Right:
Great Central Class 1, LNER Class B2, No 5424 *City of Lincoln* stands in the locomotive yard at Gorton after overhaul and repainting in LNER green with full lining c1937. This engine, the second of the class to be built, was turned out from Gorton in 1913, and withdrawn in November 1945. For most of its life it was stationed at Gorton or Immingham, but, appropriately, it had a long spell at Lincoln between 1936 and 1942.
Real Photos (1197)

Below:
The clean lines of the GCR Class 1 were repeated in the smaller-wheeled 'Glenalmond' class. The last of these to be built, in January 1915, No 5280 is evidently not long out of works after overhaul, clean and in LNER black livery lined in red. The location is Hull Dairycoates, in 1937, the engine being stationed at Colwick at the time. The later LNER style chimney adds a touch of distinction.
Crown Copyright/National Railway Museum Collection (PRW/1654)

Below right:
The third of the inside-cylindered tender classes introduced by J. G. Robinson just before World War 1, the 'Director' 4-4-0s displayed similar simplicity of outline to the 4-6-0s, although unlike the 'Sir Sam Fay' class they had valances fitted beneath the continuous splashers. Here No 6388, one of the 'D11s' built in 1924 for service in Scotland, is seen soon after delivery at Inverkeithing in charge of a stopping train from Perth to Edinburgh Waverley. The valances were removed not long afterwards, to aid access to the coupling rods.
T. G. Hepburn/Rail Archive Stephenson

5424
CITY OF LINCOLN
L N E R
6388

Above:
The doyen of LNER Class B2, known on the Great Central as the Class 1, was *Sir Fam Fay*. It is seen here in what is evidently a posed shot, which appeared as the frontispiece of the *GCR Journal* in October 1914. Two ambulance trains were provided by the Great Central, and were employed in carrying wounded soldiers between Southampton Docks and Netley Military Hospital. The location of the photograph is probably Guide Bridge, and the figures seen leaning out of the windows are not soldiers but railway staff. *Real Photos (R1593)*

Below:
'B2' 4-6-0 No 425 *City of Manchester* and a train of Pullman cars make a splendid composition. The locomotive is seen in LNER green, but retaining the large Great Central cabside numberplate and number, 425 — the tender being lettered with the original 'L&NER'. The train is the short-lived 'Sheffield Pullman' and is seen climbing the bank to Potters Bar in the summer of 1924. *F. R. Hebron/Rail Archive Stephenson*

Right:
City of Manchester, now 'B2' No 5425 and stationed at Gorton, is awaiting its next turn of duty at Manchester Central c1927; the headlamps are already positioned for a fast passenger service, probably to Sheffield. In the background is a train for Chester. *Real Photos*

Below right:
No 5424 *City of Lincoln*, is seen in Platform A at Manchester London Road station, backing on to its train which is probably bound for Cleethorpes. The engine was stationed at Gorton during the 1920s and worked mainly on cross-country services. The date is believed to be 1926, and it is interesting to note the oil tank in the tender, presumably carried during the coal strike of that year. *Real Photos*

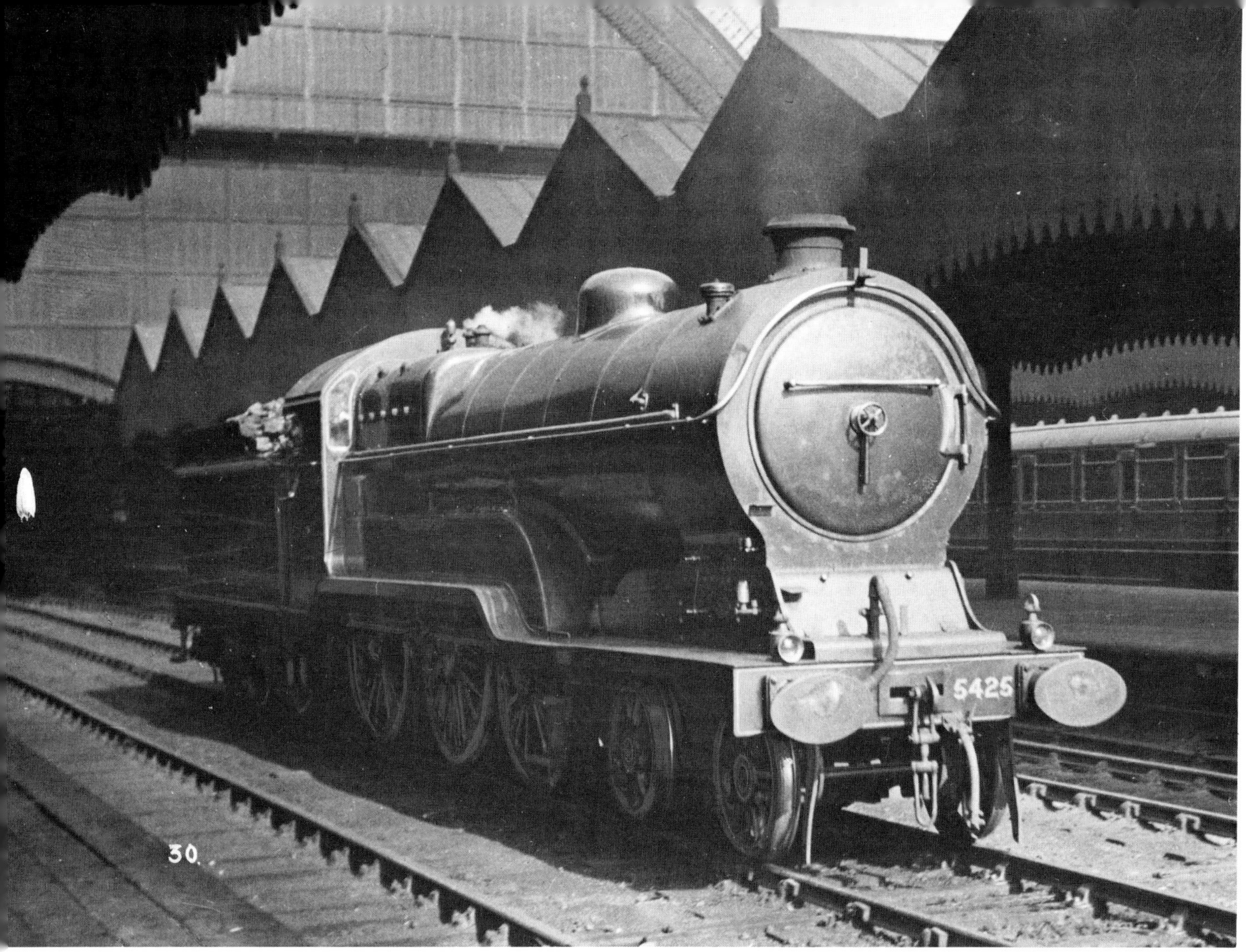
5425
30.
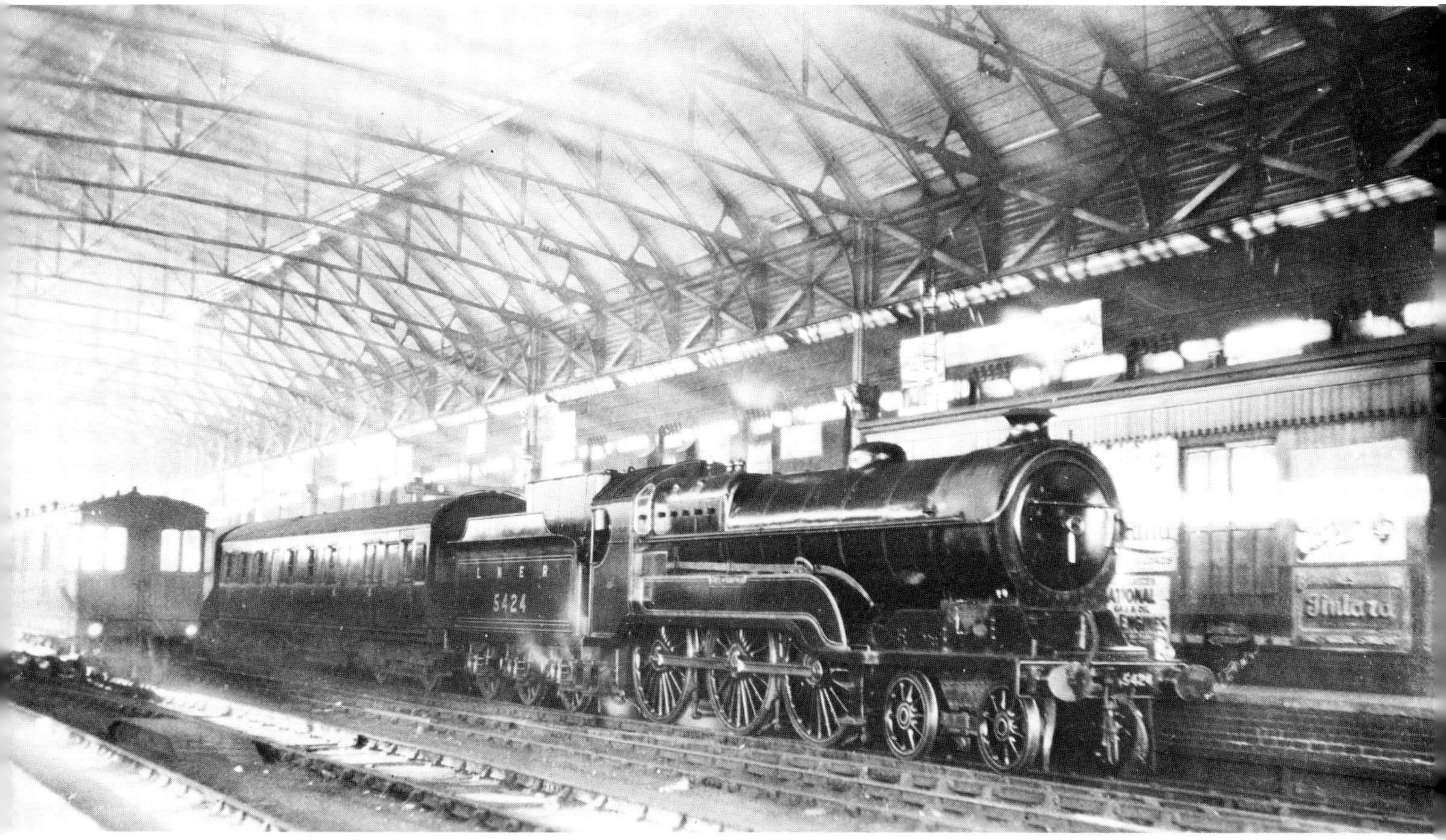
L N E R
5424
NATIONAL

Above:
No 5424 *City of Lincoln* is seen once more, in clean LNER green, with its number on the tender, working a Manchester to Cleethorpes express near Worksop in 1926. *P. Ransome-Wallis*

Below:
Whilst stationed at Immingham in the 1930s, No 5428 *City of Liverpool* was seen at King's Cross from time to time. Here it is heading an up 'Eason's Special' just south of Greenwood Box, c1930. Note the header relief valves fitted to the sides of the smokebox. At its next overhaul, No 5428 was fitted with a single Gresley-type valve behind the chimney, which at the same time was changed for one of the 'flowerpot' pattern. *C. R. L. Coles*

Above right:
Glenalmond's last shed was Darnall, Sheffield, but it found its way to Hull on 17 April 1947, where it was photographed in rather a sad state, a few months before being withdrawn. Originally GCR No 4, it became LNER No 5004 and finally No 1349. *A. F. Cook*

Below right:
The splendour of the Great Central green livery, with the company's coat-of-arms on the locomotive splashers and the tender, is well brought out in this photograph of No 279 *Earl Kitchener of Khartoum* early in its career, heading a stopping train for Manchester at Guide Bridge. *Bucknall Collection/Ian Allan Library*

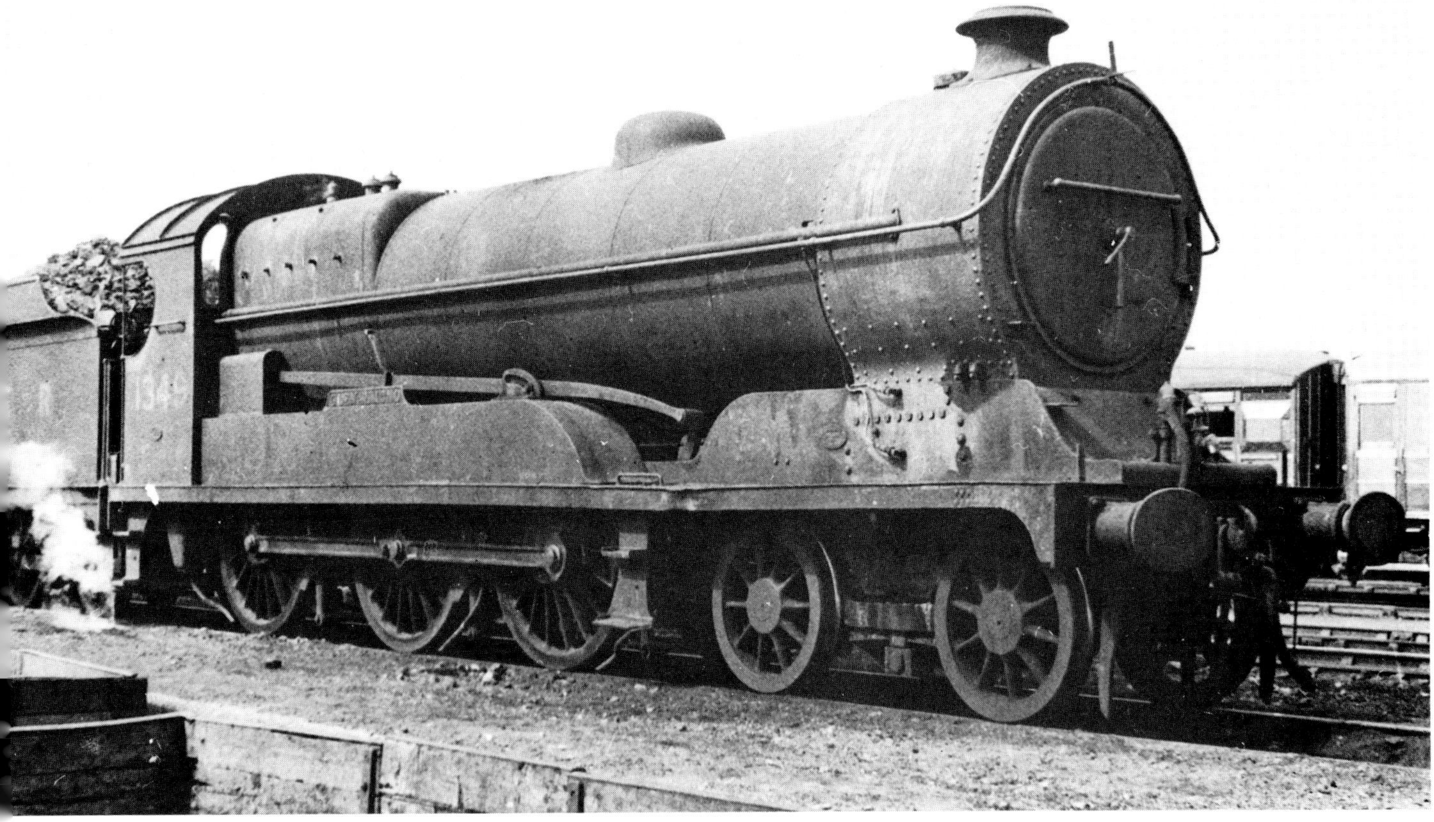

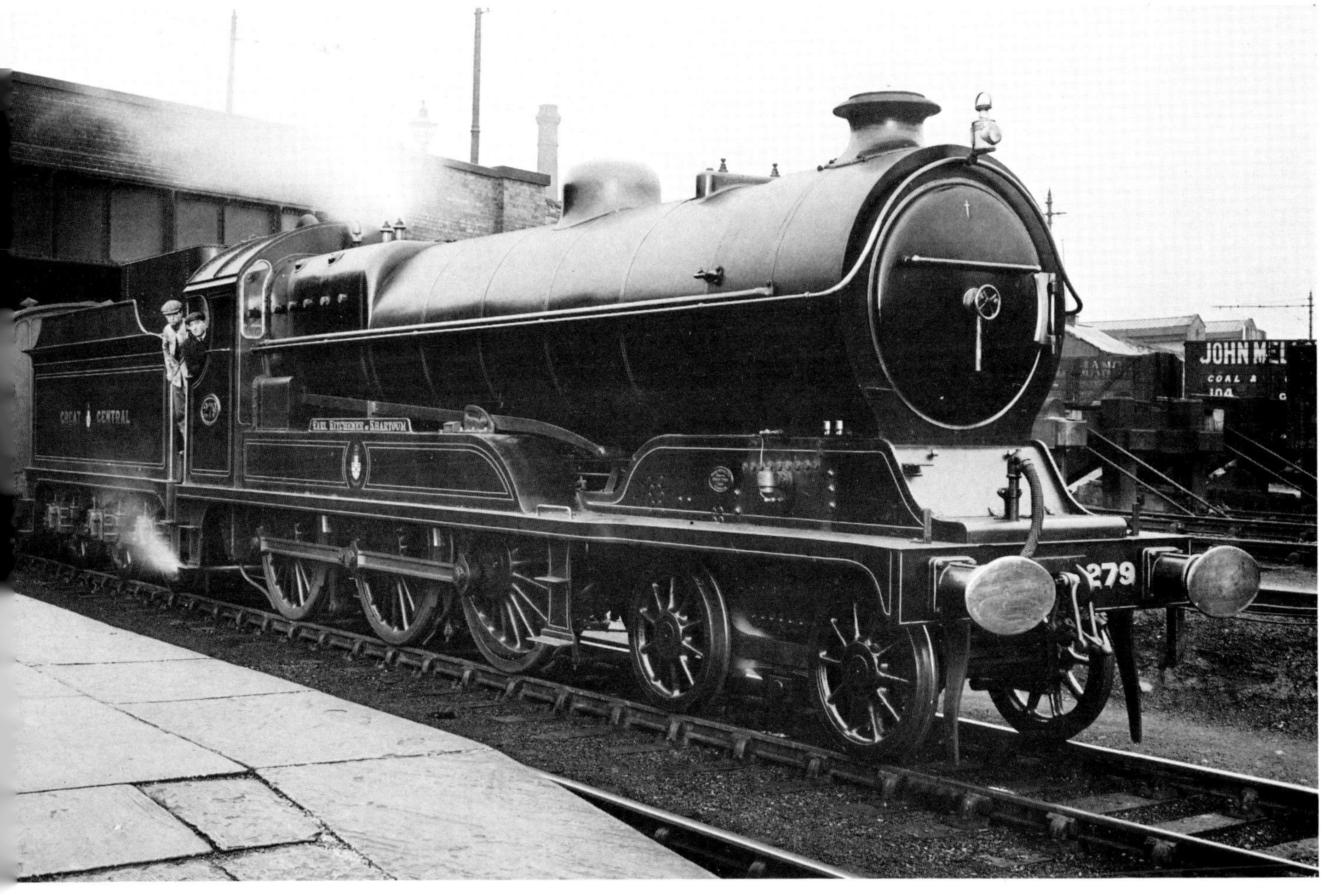
GREAT CENTRAL
EARL KITCHENER OF KHARTOUM
279

Above left:
At Nottingham Victoria on Sunday 28 March 1937, Caprotti-fitted No 6166 *Earl Haig* is awaiting a return working to Marylebone. Classified 'B3/2' after modification, the engine was later completely rebuilt by Edward Thompson and reclassified 'B3/3'. The pipe running along the side of the smokebox carries the steam supply to an ash ejector. *T. G. Hepburn/Rail Archive Stephenson*

Left:
The large 'B3' 4-6-0s were regularly used on the King's Cross Pullman services until 1927, all six being shared between King's Cross and Copley Hill, Leeds. No 6168 *Lord Stuart of Wortley* is approaching Greenwood Box on 14 August 1924 with the down 'Harrogate Pullman', strengthened by two coaches carrying Queen Mary and her retinue to Goldsborough Hall, near Harrogate, where her daughter Princess Mary lived. *F. R. Hebron/Rail Archive Stephenson*

Above:
No 6165 *Valour* was among those used on the Pullman services, but moved from King's Cross to Gorton in 1927 and is seen later that year approaching Crowden station on the descent from Woodhead, with a down express from Cleethorpes. Note the horsebox at the rear; such vehicles were not allowed on the London trains. *Real Photos (T5705)*

Below:
No 6165 *Valour* approaches Dunford Bridge on a typical Marylebone-Manchester express of the late 1920s. The first two and last two coaches are newly introduced Gresley stock with a late period GCR side corridor coach between them. *Real Photos*

Right:
Arrangements were made on Armistice Day each year for No 6165 *Valour* to work a train from Manchester to Sheffield, where a service of remembrance would be held. The locomotive's nameplates were suitably wreathed.
GCR Society Collection

Centre right:
Valour, now renumbered 1496, waits to depart from Grimsby Town with a stopping train. At this time, in 1946, the engine was allocated to Immingham, but was shortly to move to Lincoln before being withdrawn at the end of the year. *A. F. Cook*

Below:
The doyen of the 'B3' class, No 6169 *Lord Faringdon* approaches the bottleneck through Potters Bar with an up excursion on 29 April 1939. The engine was completed at Gorton in November 1917, and had an active life of 30 years before withdrawal at the end of 1947. At the time of the photograph it was stationed at Immingham and was often seen at King's Cross on workings from Grimsby, on which it was the general practice for Immingham men who knew the road to work through to London.
H. C. Doyle/
G. W. Goslin Collection

Left:
During the 1930s the 10.05pm night mail from Marylebone to Manchester and Liverpool was regularly hauled by a 'B3'. In this January 1939 photograph the engine is No 6168 *Lord Stuart of Wortley*, one of the original Caprotti conversions, and stationed at Neasden for many years. *R. F. Roberts*

Below:
No 6169 *Lord Faringdon* again, pausing at Spalding on a sunny day in the mid-1930s, with a Grimsby-King's Cross train. The train on the right would be a connecting service to March. *T. G. Hepburn/ Rail Archive Stephenson*

Above:
'B3' No 6167, bereft of nameplates, leaves Retford via the Whisker Hill curve on a Cleethorpes-Manchester stopping train on 6 May 1935. Stationed at Immingham at the time, three years later it was rebuilt with Caprotti valve gear and transferred to Neasden. Note the fish vans marshalled at the rear; it was a common practice to add a few of these to trains leaving Grimsby. *E. R. Morten*

Below:
The purposeful lines of the 'B7s' are well illustrated by this shot of No 5072 posing on the turntable at Neasden in August 1946. This was the first of the class to be built, being turned out from Gorton in 1921, but it lasted no more than 27 years, being withdrawn soon after Nationalisation. Note the massive slide bar assembly and the long piston rod. *C. C. B. Herbert*

Above:
Another example of the Grimsby practice of adding fish vans to a scheduled passenger train. 'B7' No 5482 is on an Immingham turn, hauling the midday Cleethorpes-Leicester express, leaving Worksop in 1926. The engine was built at Gorton to GCR order but not completed until the end of 1923, almost a year after the formation of the LNER. Note the larger steam chests. *P. Ransome-Wallis*

Right:
In their prime, the 'B7s' were true mixed traffic engines, regularly seeing service on secondary passenger trains. Here No 5473 is heading an excursion from Manchester, approaching Wortley in 1933. This engine was reclassified as 'B7/2', following reduction of the cab height and the fitting of cut-down boiler mountings to reduce its overall height below 13ft. *E. R. Morten*

Right:
The fireman is hard at work as 'B7' No 5469 hustles a down express into Hadley South tunnel in the late 1920s. Although no reporting number is displayed, this is unlikely to have been a scheduled service, and is probably a return excursion. *Real Photos*

4

Great Eastern 4-6-0s

In the year 1900 the Great Eastern Railway (GER) introduced a new 4-4-0 design — the first of the widely acclaimed 'Claud Hamilton' series — with driving wheels 7ft in diameter, and a tractive effort of 17,096lb. The class was subjected to a number of subsequent developments, such as the provision of Belpaire fireboxes to locomotives constructed from 1903, and trials with superheaters in 1911. Successive batches were built during the first decade of the 20th century, in a period during which train weights continued to grow. A notable example was the 'Norfolk Coast Express', which loaded up to 430 tons on its non-stop run from Liverpool Street to North Walsham, 130.1 miles in a scheduled 159min at an overall speed of 49.1mph, over a route with many sharp gradients and speed restrictions. Such loads taxed the capability of the 'Claud Hamiltons', and the Locomotive Superintendents at Stratford gave their attention to a further step forward in express motive power. The holders of this office in the final years of the Great Eastern Railway were James Holden, who retired at the end of 1907, when he was 70 years of age, and his son, S. D. Holden, who took early retirement in 1912, after only a few years in office. He was succeeded by A. J. Hill, who remained in command until the Grouping, enjoying the title of Chief Mechanical Engineer from 1915.

As the 20th century progressed, and the need for a more powerful design became urgent, it was realised that an enlarged 4-4-0 would not be feasible because of the limitation on permitted axle weight arising from the relatively light construction of the Great Eastern permanent way and many of the underbridges and height restrictions imposed by the loading gauge. Consequently, the Stratford drawing office turned their attention to a six-coupled design, and although no original details have been discovered, there is evidence that the new engine was outlined soon after S. D. Holden took office, three years before construction was commenced. A distinct similarity of lineaments with the 'Claud Hamiltons' was maintained, notably in the commodious lines of the cab and the decorative valancing over the coupled wheels. However, the new 4-6-0 emerged not merely as a stretched 'Claud', but as a design which was enlarged in almost all dimensions. The Belpaire boiler was increased in diameter from 4ft 9in to 5ft 1in, and with superheating adopted from the outset, the heating surface amounted to 1,834sq ft; boiler pressure remained at 180lb/sq in, but the grate area was increased by 18% to 26.5 sq ft. Influenced no doubt by the need to minimise the wheelbase (short turntables were another constraint on design) but also possibly by a practical view of the undulations of the GER main line, the diameter of the coupled wheels was reduced to 6ft 6in. However, the inside cylinders were substantially enlarged to 21in×28in, the result being an increase in tractive effort of over 25% to 21,969lb. Known originally as the 'S69' class, from the order number of the first batch turned out from Stratford Works, and later under LNER auspices as the 'B12' class, the new engines were often referred to as the '1500s', after the running number of the first to be completed, in December 1911. Painted in the celebrated Great Eastern ultramarine, with red lining, a plenitude of brass beading and a brass cap to the chimney, their appearance was nothing less than splendid. The '1500' was a well balanced design, which was pleasing to look at and came to be regarded with great affection by all concerned.

However, looked at critically, the class was not a great deal more powerful in terms of tractive effort than the largest 4-4-0s of the period — the Great Central 'Directors' for example — but the higher axle loading of such a 4-4-0 was out of the question. As it turned out, the adhesive weight of the 'B12s' was kept

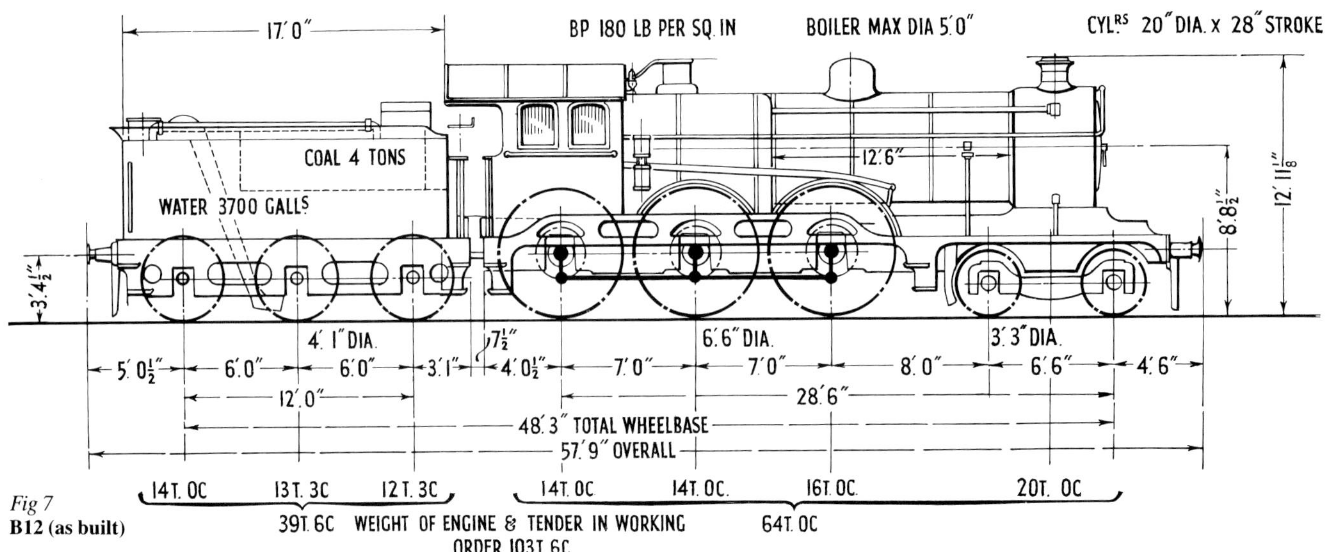

Fig 7
B12 (as built)

down to 44 tons, the maximum on one axle being no more than 15ton 13cwt. The side window cab gave the engine the appearance of being larger than it actually was, although its short overall length (for a 4-6-0) meant that the rear coupled wheel splashers intruded into the cab; thus reducing the space available to the crew. Comparison may be made with the LNWR 'Experiment' and 'Prince of Wales' classes, which also possessed inside cylinders and similar wheel diameters (actually 6ft 3in), an important distinction being the design of the firebox. A problem with any 4-6-0 was the location of the firebox and its ashpan in relation to the axles of the coupled wheels. In a case in which the wheelbase dimension was less critical than in the '1500s', sufficient length could be allowed between the middle and trailing wheels for a fairly square box to be placed between them. In the LNWR locomotives, the solution was to provide a flat grate positioned over the two axles, but Stratford looked at it differently, providing a large box by making the grate flat at the rear, but sloping it at the front to a point below the middle axle. This meant that the fireman had to throw the coal well forward, and this, added to the length of the cab and the distance from the tender to the firehole, necessitated a new technique in firing, calling for the use of special long-handled shovels.

The relatively large grate was an asset, both on the heavily loaded boat trains to and from Parkeston Quay, and on the longer Norwich turns. The boiler was free steaming, so that plenty of steam was available for the cylinders, which were rather on the large side for such a moderate sized locomotive. The 10in piston valves were placed above the cylinders and driven by Stephenson's link motion controlled by air operated reversing gear, regarded as one of the most successful of its kind ever developed, giving the option of operation by hand or air power at will. (The pump required for the Westinghouse brakes also provided the compressed air to operate the reverser. This was not to the liking of the Westinghouse Co, and special arrangements had to be made to maintain the integrity of the air supply for the braking system.)

Below:
The classic '1500' in GER days, in grey livery lined out in white with black edging, red-backed number-plate and white painted roof. No 1541 was the first to be delivered by William Beardmore in 1920. The man standing by the tender may be A. J. Hill.
LPC/Ian Allan Library (A2999)

Bottom:
The polished brass beading to the splashers was painted over when LNER green livery was first applied; later, when the number was transferred to the cabside, the beading there was removed. No 8549 is seen at Stratford, c1926. Note the Davies & Metcalfe exhaust steam ejector fitted on the framing beneath the smokebox, with its grease separator above. Some engineers claimed that this reduced fuel consumption by up to 5%. *LPC/Ian Allan Library (E10330)*

The first order was for only five locomotives, but the class was evidently satisfactorily received as 10 more were turned out in time for the summer traffic of 1913; another 24 followed, until 39 had been built at Stratford by July 1915. A delay of two years then ensued, due to the works being otherwise occupied in wartime, the two outstanding locomotives not being completed until mid-1917. (The additional one over the round 40 was in replacement of No 1506, which was in existence for only five months before being damaged beyond economic repair in a collision at Colchester in 1913; however, its tender survived to see service behind a later member of the class.)

At the end of 1918, Stratford works was heavily occupied with War Department orders, the limited railway capacity that remained available being fully employed in trying to catch up with arrears of maintenance. It was seen that after a year or so it would be possible for Stratford to complete another 10 '1500s' — these were Nos 8561-70, turned out between March and June 1920 — but if more of this urgently needed class were to be available for traffic before too long, the assistance of a contractor would be needed. So far as can be ascertained, only Vickers and Beardmore expressed any interest in this work, and the former, only for the boilers. So it was agreed that Beardmore, of Glasgow, would be given a contract for 20, although on rather loose conditions, the price negotiated being £7,750 plus 10% profit allowance, making £8,525 per locomotive. Vickers would build the boilers, and, to keep the cost down, Stratford would provide certain standard parts. The manufacturers were keen to get the order as they were changing over from Government work and had spare manufacturing capacity; on the other hand they were unpractised in locomotive building, being primarily shipbuilders, but having obtained an order for 35 2-8-0s for India felt that this could be the beginning of a series of similar contracts.

There is no indication of the Great Eastern management insisting on delivery by a particular date, but since this batch of '1500s' was allocated lower numbers than those built at Stratford, it would appear that no great delay was expected. However, progress was slow, Beardmore being troubled by the late delivery to them of special machinery needed for the contract, as well as by a strike of foundrymen. Little progress had been made by the middle of 1920, and pressure was put on Sir William Beardmore to stir things up. Eventually, the 20 locomotives were delivered, the last one in May 1921, over two years after the order was placed. Problems now arose over how much was owing, as there had been substantial increases in the costs of labour and materials, and Beardmore were looking for payment at the rate of £19,450 per locomotive — far in excess of what the GER Board expected. The books of both Beardmore and Vickers were inspected by representatives of the railway, disclosing errors in booking such that after some hard bargaining settlement was eventually reached in the sum of £17,550 each. (It would have paid the Great Eastern to wait still longer; in 1923, the Great Northern were building Pacifics for half this amount.)

An interesting variant of the class is disclosed in two Stratford drawings dated August 1914, in the possession of the National Railway Museum, which show that consideration was given to a mixed traffic version with 5ft 8in wheels. The boiler diameter and grate area were further enlarged, and an outside-cylinder version was outlined as well as the customary inside-cylinder one. However, there is no evidence to indicate that the proposal went any further than a preliminary examination. A further version exists in a proposal of c1920 for a 4-6-2T with a maximum axle loading of 20 tons, which would have severely restricted the locomotive's radius of action. It was said to have been intended for Southend line services, in which case the tank capacity of only 2,000gal might seem to be a little on the low side.

Apart from detail improvements, little alteration was made to the '1500s' until LNER days, when Gresley's interest in experimentation and Thompson's belief in the benefits of long-travel valves brought about changes in the appearance and

Bottom left:
The first of the class to be rebuilt as a 'B12/3' was No 8579, less than four years after having been turned out by Beyer Peacock in basically original form, but with Lentz poppet valves, which were replaced on rebuilding by long travel piston valves. The location is Stratford depot, in May 1932.
Crown Copyright/National Railway Museum Collection (SXB67)

Left:
Whilst still clearly a member of the 'B12' family, No 1511 shows several subtle variations from the original. The Belpaire boiler has been replaced by a round topped one of basically similar dimensions, Ross pop safety valves have been fitted, partially surrounded by a rectangular casing, and the decorative valancing beneath the running plate has been removed. Now classified 'B12/4', the engine is moving off the turntable at Kittybrewster shed.
M. H. Margerison

performance of the class. The first modification took place in February 1926 when No 8509 was fitted experimentally with a Worthington-Simpson feed water heater. This was removed three years later, but in the meantime the French ACFI system was applied to three others; this unsightly apparatus, characterised by two large heat exchanger drums fitted to the top of the boiler warmed the feed water by heat from the exhaust gases. It was evidently regarded as successful, at least in the early stages, 50 further sets of parts being purchased; as a result the majority of the class were fitted with this system. Nevertheless, subsequent experience must have indicated that maintenance costs, particularly those associated with descaling the system every few weeks because of the hard water supplies in East Anglia, more than outweighed the postulated savings in fuel and water, and the equipment was removed.

In the meantime, soon after the first experiments with feedwater heating, a more fundamental alteration was proposed, as around this period high hopes were entertained that poppet valves, derived from internal combustion engine practice, could also be applied to the steam engine, and offer as great an advantage over piston valves as these had shown over slide valves, 15 or more years earlier. Gresley was not slow to experiment with this new technique, and in 1926 a 'J20' 0-6-0 (the goods engine equivalent of the 'B12', with similar boiler and cylinders), was fitted with Lentz poppet valves, operated by oscillating cams, with some success. 'B12' No 8516 was similarly converted a few months later; this locomotive, and others fitted subsequently with Lentz valves, were reclassified 'B12/2'. No sub-classification was given to those fitted with feed water heaters. These were sometimes known as the 'Hikers', presumably because of the resemblance of the heat exchangers to a hiker's backpack.

However, whilst feedwater heaters and improved valves might bring savings in fuel and water, no significant increase in sustained power output would necessarily result. By 1927, replacement of lighter GER coaches by standard LNER vehicles and continuing increased traffic inevitably led to still higher train loads, and a shortage of sufficiently powerful locomotives brought about an operating crisis in the summer of that year. The problem was worsened by frequent overloading of the 'B12s', such that breakdowns in traffic occurred, leading to an abnormally high number of engines stopped for repair. Consequently, not only did the LNER Board give consideration to the provision of new express locomotives, but, more importantly, considered reorganising the top management structure to cope better with the diverse problems of the pre-Grouping railways forming the Southern Area of the LNER. The proposals put forward by Sir Ralph Wedgwood, the Chief General Manager, would have split the Area in two, each with a separate Divisional General Manager, but in the event the problem was resolved by maintaining the single Area, but appointing two Superintendents to run the railway — one for the Western Section (GC and GN) and another for the Eastern Section (GE). These appointments were paralleled in the Locomotive Running Department, and in the representatives of the Chief Mechanical Engineer, although in the latter case it was a change in designation only, as C. W. Glaze and been in charge at Stratford, with the title of Mechanical Engineer, since he had succeeded A. J. Hill at the Grouping. However, more than managerial change was needed if the Eastern Section trains were to be run efficiently. Gresley was aware of the problem and had requested the Doncaster drawing office to work up a 4-6-0 design with three cylinders all driving on to the same axle and his conjugated mechanism for operating the valves of the middle

Above and right:
Two short-lived variations of LNER numbering are shown. No 1535_E (note also the 'L&NER') is seen at Stratford in 1923, and No 7476 (previously No 8562, and later No 1562) at March in September 1945. The former is fitted with the 'Superior' tube cleaning apparatus, and the prominent steam pipe on the latter is connected to the exhaust steam injector.
LPC/Ian Allan Library (10534); R. G. H. Simpson

cylinder. It was a have a tractive effort of 25,000lb, a 15% improvement on that of the 'B12s'. At the same time Stratford drawing office was at work on a 2-6-4T intended primarily for Southend line trains, which would have a 'K2' front end, 'J39' boiler and 6ft 2in wheels. In fact a batch of 12 of these tank engines was included in the 1928 locomotive building programme, at an estimated cost of £6,220 each. (This was an interesting throwback to the 4-6-2T proposal of 1920.)

Matters had reached a critical stage by the end of the summer of 1927, without any sign of the new engines appearing, so much so that the Chief Officers concerned concluded that the best solution would be to build a further 20 'B12s' as a matter of urgency, and cancel the 2-6-4Ts. In any case, the operating department were not in favour of this new class, preferring the more generally useful 4-6-0 tender engines, which would not suffer from the operating limitations imposed by a tank engine design. Moreover, the recent Sevenoaks disaster on the Southern Railway, involving a similar type of locomotive, had put in doubt the use of such engines on fast services.

Consequently, on 26 January 1928, the Chief General Manager submitted a recommendation to a joint meeting of the Locomotive and Traffic Committees of the Board that 20 'B12s' should be built. However, the Directors did not agree; only 10 were authorised, and the CME was instructed to produce an improved 4-6-0 as soon as possible (this was to be the 'B17' class, discussed in Chapter 5); but because both Doncaster and Darlington were occupied with other work, the 10 'B12s' were put out to tender. There was plenty of spare capacity in the private locomotive works at the time, and seven quotations were received, the lowest being from Robert Stephenson and Co, at £5,943 each — interestingly, less than the estimate for the 2-6-4Ts to be built in the Company's works. However, Beyer Peacock could offer much better delivery than Stephenson, and so they were awarded the contract, at £5,975 per locomotive delivered to Gorton, with a penalty clause, insisted upon by Gresley, of £25 per engine delivered behind schedule. This was in fact invoked, as most of the batch were delivered too late to take part in the summer traffic of 1928, a total penalty of £525 being applied. However, the matter had been complicated by the CME's requirement that Lentz poppet valves should be fitted in place of the piston valves shown on the original drawings supplied by Stratford for Peacock's use. This modification appears not to have been taken into consideration in their estimate, nor in their calculation of delivery times, and consequently the manufacturers made a counterclaim on the LNER for the additional costs involved. At that period Beyer Peacock had Sir Sam Fay as Chairman and R. H. Whitelegg, previously of the Glasgow & South Western Railway, as General Manager, so that they were fully aware of how a railway company dealt with its contractors; also, of course, the officers concerned were well known personally to Gresley.

Beyer Peacock's records of June 1928 include a note that the engines were to have Lentz valves, indicating that they were aware of the modification at that time, but perhaps relying on the cost of the valves being regarded as an 'extra', whereas the LNER looked at it differently. Matters dragged on for some months, as on 10 October 1929 Sir Sam Fay wrote in the following terms:

Dear Gresley,
Adverting to our conversation upon the loss sustained by Beyer Peacock & Co in the building of 10 engines for your company, the subject has again been before my Board, which is composed of men all of whom have had experience in contracts. They expressed surprise at the view taken by you of the claim made for a portion of the loss, which was not due in any way to the fault of Beyer Peacock & Co.

The fact that other manufacturers gave in tenders somewhat similar in price to that of Beyer Peacock & Co does not mean that a claim would not have been made by them if they had secured the contract. I may mention that the diagram accompanying your invitation to tender is very different to the photograph you showed me. The former is dated 1913.

Under the circumstances I am sorry to say that we cannot let the matter rest. No manufacturer could possibly live under such conditions and I must ask you to please go into the question again with a view to the meeting of our claim.

Yours faithfully

Sam Fay

After getting nowhere in correspondence, Court proceedings were threatened by Beyer Peacock against the LNER for the sum of £3,000, but in the end settlement was achieved privately for half this amount, the LNER at the same time dropping their penalty claim. At this distance in time it is impossible to say what went wrong but there were evidently misunderstandings, and no doubt sore heads, on both sides. It is a strange coincidence that, recalling the Beardmore contract of 1919, the two occasions on which 'B12s' had been put out to tender both led to serious disagreement between the railway and its suppliers.

The Lentz valve engines were said at first to be more sprightly, and to run considerably longer between heavy repairs, than the piston-valved originals. Unfortunately however the poppet valves did not live up to expectations, although a further six locomotives were converted, the last in April 1930. Experience in practice led to camshafts twisting and, more seriously, cylinder blocks cracking, resulting in a requirement for premature and expensive replacements. In contrast to Chapelon's experience in France, the oscillating cam drives were not successful in applications on the LNER; excess backlash was one of the contributory problems and later experiments with other classes concentrated on rotary driven cams to operate the valves. Consequently all the Lentz valve engines were reconverted to the original piston valve design after only three years in service, the first being No 8577 of the Beyer Peacock batch.

Edward Thompson, later to succeed Gresley as Chief Mechanical Engineer of the LNER, was active on the Great Eastern section at this period, having been promoted from Carriage and Wagon Works Manager at York to be Assistant Mechanical Engineer at Stratford, in 1927, succeeding C. W. Glaze as Mechanical Engineer in March 1930. By then improvements had been made to the GE section permanent way, sufficient to allow some relaxation in maximum axle weights, at least on the main lines, and as a result a radical updating of the original 'B12' design was introduced. This featured not only redesigned valve movements, with maximum travel increased from 4$\frac{3}{16}$in to 6$\frac{1}{16}$in, but also a larger boiler, 5ft 6in in diameter, and with front end details improved. The boiler barrel was a shortened version of that of the newly introduced 'B17', and the firebox was completely redesigned, being longer and shallower than the original, and round-topped instead of Belpaire; the grate area was enlarged to a respectable 31sq ft. With a slightly increased facility for superheat, the total heating surface went up to 1,874sq ft, but without alteration to the cylinder dimensions or boiler pressure, the tractive effort remained unchanged at 21,969lb.

The first of the class to benefit from the lengthened valve travel was No 8559, converted in December 1930, and the first to be rebuilt with the new boiler was No 8579, of the Beyer Peacock batch, in May 1932. A feature of the 10 built in 1928 had been the absence of the decorative valancing over the coupled wheels, and this was also removed from earlier engines as they were rebuilt. Furthermore, the larger diameter boiler called for smaller mountings, and Ross pop instead of Ramsbottom safety valves, whilst the shorter cab necessitated by the longer firebox led to a small segment of splasher appearing over each of the trailing coupled wheels. All in all the improvements resulted in a complete change in the appearance of the class — sleek lines, in the Gresley tradition, replacing the ornate detail of the original Holden design of 20 years earlier. The larger boiler increased the weight of the rebuilds by 6½ tons to 69ton 10cwt, and although the maximum axle load was increased, it was still no more than 17 tons — a figure acceptable by the Engineer for all but the lesser branches of the GE section. This comprehensive reconstruction was judged to be successful, with savings in fuel and water of up to 20%, and eventually no fewer than 54 of the class were converted in this way, mostly between 1932 and 1938, but the last as late as January 1944. The rebuilds were classified as 'B12/3', but one important feature remained in that they kept their short GER pattern tenders, enabling them to be accommodated on a 50ft turntable.

A final variation of the class appeared later in its life, after several 'B12s' in original condition had been transferred to the Northern Scottish Area, where severe weight limitations continued, prohibiting the employment of heavier locomotives, including the rebuilt 'B12/3s'. Consequently, as replacement boilers became needed from 1943 onwards, a new design of boiler to LNER standards was introduced. The main dimensions remained the same as those of the original members of the class,

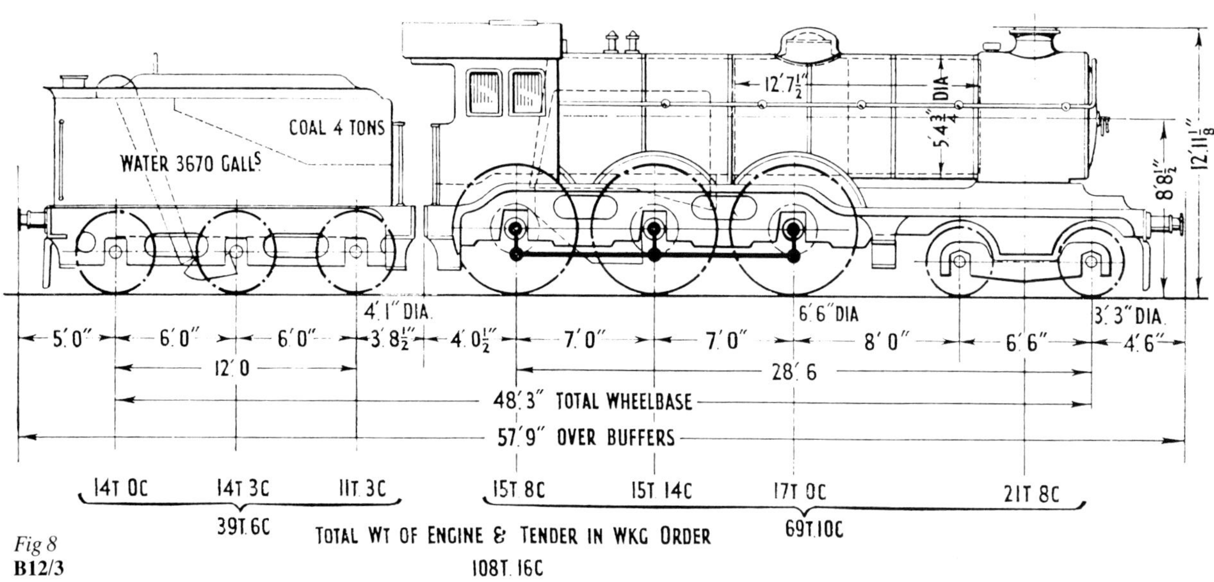

Fig 8
B12/3

but with some alterations to the tubing arrangements, and of course, provision of a round-topped firebox. Nine of its class were rebuilt in this way, and classified 'B12/4', but 16 (all but one in Scotland) remained virtually in their original condition until withdrawal. It must be remembered however that the softer Scottish water was much more conducive to lengthy boiler life than the hard water of East Anglia.

Turning now to performance, the 1912 timing of the Hook of Holland boat train over the 68.9 miles from Liverpool Street to Parkeston Quay was 87min with a train of relatively lightweight coaches hauled by a 'Claud Hamilton' 4-4-0. In a trial run with 330 tons the first of the new 4-6-0s achieved a start-to-stop time of 75min, with a minimum speed of 46mph up Brentwood Bank. As a result, 5min were cut from the schedule, it having been ascertained that the '1500s' were able to pass Shenfield in 3min less time than was customary with the 'Claud Hamiltons'. No 1500's achievement represented possibly the best-ever performance over this difficult route, but the 82min timing, with a load regularly reaching 400 tons, at an average speed of 50.4mph, required sterling locomotive work to achieve punctuality. The 'Hook Continental' as the train was titled, was an early candidate for new stock under the auspices of the LNER, 10 new 61ft 6in coaches of standard teak construction being built for the service in 1924; with two Pullman cars in addition, the gross weight was 465 tons — and further coaches were added on occasion. This was not all, however, as the train was vacuum braked, the ejectors for this system giving rise to a heavier demand for steam than the pump for the Westinghouse air brake, which had been the Great Eastern standard, whilst in the winter months steam heating added considerably to the drain on the engine's boiler. As a result, the schedule was later eased to the previous 87min.

Cecil J. Allen commenced his railway career as a civil engineer on the Great Eastern Railway and, as might be expected, recorded several journeys behind 'B12s', including a number of footplate runs. One of the best of these was in 1922, when the down 'Hook Continental', consisting of 10 GER coaches and two Pullman cars, grossing some 420 tons, reached Parkeston Quay in 81min 5sec, almost 1min early, the run being free from out-of-course checks. Allen repeated this trip a short while later, enjoying a run which he rightly assessed as one of his finest on this train; the locomotive was No 1566, built at Stratford in 1920. A start 1min late gave an additional impetus to the footplate crew, who were severely checked at the foot of Brentwood Bank, but nevertheless achieved an arrival at Parkeston Quay 45sec early.

After allowing for signal checks, Allen computed the net time to be no more than 79¾min.

In passing, it is an interesting commentary on the standards of the period to note the precision of the train timings. An arrival at Parkeston Quay at exactly 8.52pm represented a fine performance, but the train to the quayside was only a part of the overall journey to a Continental destination, the overnight schedule of the ferry being by no means timed so closely. To have eased the time of the train so that it arrived at 8.55pm, or even 9.00pm, would have made no material addition to the time of arrival at the Hook, whilst the savings in terms of lower coal consumption, as the locomotive would not have had to be worked so hard, would have been significant. The answer of course lies in the highly competent attitude of the contemporary railwaymen, from operational management to footplate crew, determined to run their part of the journey efficiently at high speed, and achieving recognition, if not necessarily from the passengers, at least from their fellow professionals in Britain and abroad. However, the *up* train carrying passengers off the early morning arrivals from the Continent was not so sharply timed, no doubt because of the potential conflict with the commuter traffic into Liverpool Street. In the summer of 1938, the up 'Hook Continental' was allowed 98min on weekdays, but on Sundays, when the line was less congested, the schedule was only 90min, including a conditional stop at Colchester.

After the LNER had provided a further new set of coaches for the 'Hook Continental' in 1938, the schedule was relaxed to 90min, but the new train of 12 coaches, including two Pullman cars, grossed up to 520 tons, and for this the 'B12/3s' were preferred to the 'B17s'. Although over a relatively short distance, the fireman was heavily engaged for virtually the whole of the 1½hr journey and strict regard had to be kept to passing times, as if time were lost in the early stages there was little opportunity to regain it later.

Of course the boat expresses were only one use to which the 'B12s' were put. For many years the class was responsible for the main workings to Norwich via Ipswich, and later via Cambridge, as well as to the Norfolk coast resorts. As an example of their earlier exploits, records exist of a run on the 'Norfolk Coast Express' with 360 tons, in which the 130.1 miles to North Walsham took 153min 9sec, or 150min net of delays, an average of over 50mph. The additional 30 locomotives built by the GER after World War 1 brought the total at Grouping to 70, so providing cover for the important services of the period, as well as extending the sphere of operation of the class, as bridge and track conditions permitted. Clacton and Walton were brought within their ambit in 1927, whilst after the Beyer Peacock batch had been delivered in 1928 they were seen at Southend as a matter of course. On the wider scene, one or more were regularly stationed at Gorton in 1927, and worked through from Manchester to Ipswich (a distance of 216 miles) — a considerable contrast to the 60 miles of the London boat expresses. However, the schedule of the 'North Country Continental', as the train was unofficially termed, was less demanding. From the end of 1928, the 'B12s' were gradually replaced on this working by the new 'B17s'.

Post-Grouping conditions involved the temporary employment of individual members of the class at other locations, such as Copley Hill, to work stopping trains between Leeds and Doncaster, whilst each of the Beyer Peacock batch of 1928 was stationed for a time at Gorton for acceptance trials and running in; sometimes they were used on trains to Sheffield and beyond. On occasions in the 1920s 'B12s' helped out on the London Extension of the Great Central, the GE section loaning complete trains for excursions to the British Empire Exhibition which was staged at Wembley in 1924 and 1925, and for the FA and other Cup Finals held there each year. The first recorded occurrence was as early as April 1923, when No 1554 worked a Cup Final special. On other occasions large circular headboards were featured on excursions carrying Rolls-Royce employees

Above:
In an early trial of feedwater heating, a Worthington-Simpson heater and pump were fitted to No 8509 in 1926. After three years the apparatus was removed and later replaced by the ACFI system, which in turn was dismantled in 1935 when the engine was rebuilt as a 'B12/3'. *Ian Allan Library*

Left:
ACFI-fitted No 8510 and the down 'Eastern Belle' are passing through Brentwood station in June 1933. Note the material in place for the widening to four tracks. *Real Photos*

from Derby, and Boots staff from Nottingham, headed by Nos 8532 and 8507 respectively. Such were the advantages of effective collaboration within the Southern Area of the newly formed LNER.

A trial which was to have important results took place in 1926 when a 'B12' was tried successfully on the Great North of Scotland (GN of S) system, where the replacement of obsolete 4-4-0s was a matter of urgency. However, the shortage of express locomotives on the Great Eastern section was such that the Southern Area management resisted pressure for the permanent transfer of any 'B12s' until more 'B17s' had been built. The eventual availability of these new engines then led to the transfer of the first five 'B12s', Nos 8500-04, to Kittybrewster in 1931-32. Others followed at intervals, until by the end of the war no fewer than 25 were stationed in Scotland. They came to be used on all the GN of S main lines, including the Deeside line to Ballater, as well as on fish trains from the small North Sea ports into Aberdeen. They proved to be ideal for the duties involved, and once the local crews had become accustomed to the new techniques of driving and firing, were well liked by the enginemen; a few spent more time in Scotland than they did in their native East Anglia. The schedules were not onerous, nor were there long non-stop runs on the GN of S, whose main line was described by a Stratford fitter sent to Inverurie to train the local men in the maintenance of the new engines, as 'an endless succession of Manningtree curves'. On a trip behind No 8503, with 270 tons, a recorder noted that by good uphill work 2min were gained on the 12.5 miles between Keith and Huntly (schedule 18min at 41.7mph) but a minute was lost between Inverurie and Dyce as the engine seemed to be dawdling. 'What a contrast', said the commentator, 'with the "Hook Continental" '. The 'B12s' were also used on summer excursions on the West Highland line, and were noted between Glasgow and Edinburgh, although such sightings probably occurred just after the engine concerned had been overhauled at Cowlairs, rather than as a regular working.

The 'B12/3' rebuilds were regarded in certain circumstances as the equals of the 'B17s'; indeed, in the later 1930s, when the 'Hook Continental' was loaded to 520 tons or more, a 'B12/3' was the preferred locomotive, although the timing had by then been relaxed to the round 90min. Moreover, although the 'B17s' were generally used on the heaviest of the longer turns, such as the London-Norwich expresses, Cecil J. Allen had described two runs in which 'B12/3s' gave excellent performances on trains from Ipswich. With 11 coaches weighing 355 tons gross, No 8544 took no more than 74½min net for the 68.8 miles to Liverpool Street; in BR days a 'Britannia' would have been allowed 83min. On another occasion No 8535, with a down train of 10 coaches, achieved 90mph just before an emergency stop was made at Diss, the start-to-stop time from Ipswich being 26min for the 26.3 miles. However, the rebuilds were not normally used on the 'North Country Continental', 'B17s' being favoured for this long distance lodging turn.

Evidence is available of the ability of the 'B12s' to achieve sustained high speeds. In the first week of July 1936, a trial was conducted to verify the feasibility of a 2hr schedule to Norwich. A six-coach train ran the outward journey in 2hr, and could have returned in the same time had not a lengthy halt been imposed at Ipswich to allow the road to scheduled services. Also, in the same summer, No 8558, with the customary seven Pullman cars of the 'Eastern Belle', reached Norwich in 125min, with a top speed of 81mph at Manningtree.

In prewar days, 'B12s' were rarely seen on the Great Northern section south of Doncaster, and although it was the practice to allocate a small number to Cambridge and use them on such trains as the Buffet Car expresses to Liverpool Street, few workings on the equivalent trains to King's Cross have been

Below:
After completion of the widening, No 8508 is climbing Brentwood Bank with the 'Flushing Continental'. The train is made up of Gresley stock together with Pullman cars, and is travelling on the new down fast line, the original two tracks now taking the slow traffic. *Real Photos (T5220)*

recorded, these generally having been in the hands of Ivatt Atlantics, assisted by the two 'Royal Clauds' Nos 8783 and 8787. After Nationalisation, a few 'B12s' found their way to Grantham, where they were mainly employed on stopping trains, but they were known to have travelled to York and Bridlington on excursion workings and, in an emergency, one was even recorded as having reached King's Cross at the head of the prestige 'West Riding' express.

As additional 'B17s' were built for Great Eastern services, the 'B12s' took over more duties, such as trains to Clacton and other seaside towns, from the 'Claud Hamiltons', and they were also allocated to March for work on the GN/GE Joint Line between

Above:
'B12' No 8553 is leaving Audley End tunnel with an up Cambridge line train c1930. In the earliest version of the post-1928 numbering, the number was seen on the cabside above the beading, which remained in place. Later the beading was removed, and the number was repositioned centrally. *LPC/Ian Allan Library*

Below:
The down Harwich to Liverpool boat train, unofficially known as the 'North Country Continental' leaving Worksop headed by 'B12' No 8535, c1928. The engine was based at Ipswich at the time, and worked through to Manchester, sharing the duty with a Gorton 'B12' on alternate days. *Crown Copyright/ National Railway Museum Collection (PRW 508)*

March and Doncaster. After Nationalisation, with the allocation to the Great Eastern of 'Britannia' Pacifics and large numbers of 'B1s', many of the 'B12s' continued to be found at Stratford, where they took over the exclusive working of the Southend line trains. A few were transferred to South Lynn or Yarmouth Beach, some being fitted with tablet exchange equipment for working on the Midland & Great Northern Joint Line.

The 'B12's' characteristic of relatively high power output for low axle weight provided them with a new sphere of operations in wartime, namely working ambulance trains — not only on their own ground but also on the lines of other systems. This was particularly the case in 1939-45, when they were used to haul trains of US-built coaches fitted with air brakes, the dual Westinghouse/vacuum systems of the 'B12s' being a further aid to their wide route availability. In this connection they were often to be found on the Great Western and Southern systems in West and South-West England. No 8549 is on record as having been stationed at Templecombe in 1944, and No 7479 at Bournemouth, together with their trains, being used for the conveyance of American servicemen wounded in the Normandy landings. On another occasion a 'B12/3' is recalled heading westward from Cardiff, piloted by a GWR Mogul.

Apart from No 1506 (the Colchester victim of 1913), the first 'B12' to be scrapped was the still unrebuilt No 8551, in 1947. Those transferred to Scotland were amongst the earliest to be withdrawn, whilst most of the 'B12/3s' continued in service until well into the 1950s. The last to go was No 8572, then renumbered 61572, which was saved from the scrapheap by being purchased by the North Norfolk Railway. It is now under restoration at Weybourne by a team led by Bill Harvey, but the engine was in a very run-down state and funds are needed to complete the work.

The class was numbered from 1500 to 1570 in Great Eastern days, and with the exception of the prematurely withdrawn No 1506, were renumbered from 8500 to 8570 by the LNER who added Nos 8571-8580 in 1928. By an interesting piece of sympathetic treatment the 1946 LNER renumbering brought them back to their original sequence, although an interim renumbering intended to clear a large block of numbers for the 'B1' class led to a few being numbered in a group between 7415 and 7494. Only those built before 1915 were seen in ultramarine, others being painted a mid-grey until LNER green began to be applied after the Grouping. One of the class was amongst the engines displayed at Marylebone in February 1923 to assist the LNER Board in taking a decision on the new company's livery, No 1534 being splendidly turned-out in apple green, with all its brasswork highly polished. Being large-wheeled 4-6-0s, the class escaped the 1928 strictures which sharply reduced the number of classes retaining green livery, although strangely Inverurie painted most of its fleet in lined black. During World War 2, unrelieved black was the norm, but a few were to be seen in LNER green once more in the immediate postwar years. Consistent with Great Eastern policy (except for four engines, the best known of which were *Petrolea* and *Claud Hamilton*) none of the 'B12s' was ever given a name, the 10 built in 1928 — together with the 'Hush-hush' No 10000 — being the only LNER engines built specifically for express workings to remain nameless.

When the '1500s' were first seen, the brass beading was omitted from the cabside; this displeased S. D. Holden, who ordered that subsequent engines should have the curved splasher beading repeated on the cabside. To comply with this, it was necessary for the numberplate to be reduced in size. In 1920, as a result of adopting a train control system which called for the easier identification of locomotives, large numbers were painted on the tenders and the company's initials were omitted. The LNER restored the letters to the tender, at first together with the number. However, from 1929 numbers were transferred to the cabside, which resulted in Holden's beading being removed.

As a final comment on the original GER design, it is appropriate once more to quote Cecil J. Allen. In the *Railway Magazine* of January 1920 he wrote that 'the 1500 class possess a limited boiler mated to large cylinders for tractive purposes. There is no shortage of steam because of the provision of a large and well designed firebox, so that the engines in question steam with an ease which is quite disproportionate to what might be expected.' This tribute was echoed by all railwaymen who claim to have experience of them.

Below:
Nicely turned-out 'B12' No 8507 takes water at Spalding, c1931. Judging from the roof boards it is working the down boat train from Harwich. This divided at Lincoln, the main part going to Liverpool and the remainder north to York. The engine's number has been transferred to the cabside, above the beading, but the 'LNER' on the tender remains in small (7½in) letters. The engine on the right is 'D15/2' No 8861.
L&GRP, courtesy David & Charles (10396)

Above:
The 'B12s' sent to Scotland sometimes operated in pairs on the fish trains working into Aberdeen from the north. No 1563 (in black livery) is piloting No 1543 (in green), seen passing Kittybrewster in 1947. Both engines had been transferred to the Northern Scottish Area in 1939, and remained there until withdrawal in 1953. *Crown Copyright/National Railway Museum Collection (PRW 3483)*

Below:
In early BR days, 'B12' No 61502 is seen pulling away from Aberdeen station with the 6.10pm stopping train to Keith on 29 August 1953. The locomotive, one of the first of the class to be built, spent 19 years in its native East Anglia and 23 in Scotland. *Brian Morrison*

Left:
'B12s' stationed at Kittybrewster were occasionally loaned to Eastfield shed, Glasgow to work excursions to Oban via the Crianlarich spur and the LMS line. No 8548 is seen leaving Crianlarich Lower on 4 July 1938 with a train of green and cream tourist stock.
G. W. Goslin Collection

Centre left:
The popularity of buffet cars led to their inclusion in an increasing number of trains serving the East Anglian resorts. 'B12/3' No 8564 is heading an up buffet car train from Ipswich near Chadwell Heath in 1939.
Real Photos (23718)

Bottom left:
Several 'B12/3s' were employed on ambulance train duty on the Great Western during the last years of World War 2, the engine and coaches staying together for long periods. Here, No 8557 is piloted by GWR 2-6-0 No 5303, at Kennington Junction, Oxford, on 26 June 1944. The train would have been carrying wounded servicemen to Wheatley Military Hospital. *R. H. G. Simpson*

Above right:
It was unusual to see a pair of 'B12/3s' on the same train, but here No 1565, in postwar green livery, is piloting an unidentifiable member of the same class hauling the down 'Scandinavian' boat train on 9 July 1947. The location is Wrabness, on the Harwich branch. *C. C. B. Herbert*

Right:
At the beginning of the BR period, in the summer of 1948, but not yet bearing indications of its new ownership, 'B12/3' No 1516 leaves Shenfield with an up slow train for Liverpool Street. One wonders what adverse effect the corrosive exhaust of steam locomotives had on the overhead catenary. *P. Ransome-Wallis*

Above:
Towards the end of their life, a small number of 'B12/3s' were at work on the East Coast main line between Grantham and Peterborough. No 61574 is seen in August 1953, heading an up stopping train in Saltersford Cutting. (This train was the successor to the old GNR up 'Parly', which was often used as a running-in turn for engines overhauled at Doncaster.)
John F. Clay

Below and right:
Two studies of LNER 4-6-0s after 10 years of BR ownership, waiting their next turn of duty. (Below) On 5 September 1959, 'B12/3' No 61533 comes off shed at Cambridge. This engine had recently completed a 10-year stint on the Midland & Great Northern Joint Line, but had only two months to go before withdrawal. (Right) The engine sidings at the down side of Ipswich station, in the summer of 1958. 'B12/3' No 61576 (built 1928) and 'B1' No 61223 (built 1947) were by now used indiscriminately on secondary trains, 'Britannia' Pacifics having taken over the main passenger services.
S. Rickard/M. Dunnett

'B12/3' No 61555 is seen at the head of the 10.50am Liverpool Street-Cambridge on 29 August 1952. *R. E. Vincent*

5

Gresley 4-6-0s

The LNER Board considered their Continental traffic to be of great importance, and an early decision was taken to build a new train for the 'Hook Continental', the company's prestige overnight service to the Hook of Holland, departing from Liverpool Street at 8.30 each evening and connecting with the steamer at Parkeston Quay. This represented a formidable challenge to the locomotive power available, although the distance was no more than 68.9 miles. Moreover, new coaching stock provided for other Great Eastern services was also built to the heavier LNER standards, although on the ordinary trains the coach length was 52ft 6in instead of the usual 61ft 6in of the stock built for the boat trains and for general service elsewhere on the system. The main reason for this was the sharp curves at certain Great Eastern station platforms.

The stud of 70 'B12' 4-6-0s, still in original condition, were capable engines within their limitations, but as discussed in Chapter 4 a requirement emerged for more powerful locomotives to take the brunt of the heavier trains. Also, the GE Section was in need of new engines to replace older life-expired 2-4-0s and 4-4-0s, although this problem was alleviated to an extent by the transfer of 20 ex-Great Northern 'K2' 2-6-0s, replaced on that section by new 'K3s' entering service. The 'K2s' were found to be particularly useful on Southend line trains, and for excursion and relief passenger workings on summer Saturdays, but they were unsuitable for the faster expresses. Consequently, it was made clear to the Chief Mechanical Engineer that a new class of locomotive would be needed, more powerful than the '1500s', yet within the limits of axle loading

permitted by the Civil Engineer. Construction of new locomotives would release '1500s' from the more important duties, so that they could transfer to lesser services and allow obsolete four-coupled engines to be withdrawn.

A medium powered 4-4-0, the 'D49' — otherwise known as the 'Shire' class — had been introduced to Gresley's specification in 1927, but this was insufficiently powerful for the tasks in mind on the Great Eastern, as well as having an unacceptable maximum axle load of 21¼ tons. Nor could a Pacific be used, and no pre-Grouping class appeared strong and yet light enough, although a Scottish 'D11', No 6399 *Allan-Bane* was loaned to Stratford in January 1927 in exchange for 'B12' No 8526, which was on trial at Kittybrewster. The 'Director' did not stay longer than a week or so, and the Engineer would surely have placed an embargo on it as soon as he learned about its visit. So, the opportunity presented itself for a new 4-6-0 to be designed in the CME's Department, and Gresley concluded that this would be of sufficient size and importance to warrant the application of his preference for the three-cylinder method of propulsion, with the drive for the valves of the inside cylinders derived from that of those outside, by the employment of his '2 to 1' system of linkages. Moreover, Gresley also specified a further principle, that all three cylinders should drive on to the same coupled axle.

Impetus for a three-cylinder design had been given by the Report of the Bridge Stress Committee, which pointed to the advantages in the reduced level of hammerblow of a three-cylinder design over a corresponding one with two cylinders, envisaging less propensity to damage to track and underbridges. However, whilst acknowledging this as a principle, the matter rested on agreement between the CME and the Civil Engineer. In the event it seems that the Engineer was prepared to accept a maximum axle load of 17 tons, an increase of 14% over the 15ton 13cwt of the 'B12s'. So, Doncaster drawing office was put to work on a 6ft 8in 4-6-0 with a tractive effort of 25,000lb, and with all three cylinders driving on to the centre coupled axle.

This proved to be more difficult than was at first thought, the initial design being rejected as being too heavy, having 17 tons on the bogie and 19 tons on each driving axle. Moving the coupled wheels further back, so transferring weight on to the bogie, only partially alleviated the difficulty as the lengthened engine, plus a standard 4,200gal tender, was too long, as further constraints emerged in the shortness of the Great Eastern turntables and the lay-byes at Liverpool Street station. As discussed in Chapter 4, pressure for the new engines built up,

Below:
The first four 'Sandringhams' sent out from Hyde Park Works by NBL had their nameplates on the leading splashers, in the same fashion as the 'Royal Scots'. This was not to the LNER's liking, and the plates were refixed to the centre splashers before the engines were placed in service. No 2800 was photographed by NBL before being handed over; note the maker's plate on the smokebox, and the owner's plate on the cab.
The Mitchell Library, Glasgow

Above:
After a decision had been taken to name one of the 'B17s' *The Suffolk Regiment*, experimental nameplates of alternative designs were cast and fitted temporarily to No 2803. In this version, the plate incorporates the insignia of the regiment above the name, but the final decision was to place it on the face of the splasher. The name was actually conferred on the newly-built No 2845, at a ceremony on 22 June 1935.
Crown Copyright/National Railway Museum Collection (SX 1620A)

Left:
Originally named *Norwich City* and now in its new role as *East Anglian*, No 2859 is on the turntable at Liverpool Street in preparation for the return working of the newly introduced express of the same name, on 28 September 1937.
LCGB/Ken Nunn Collection

and as an emergency measure 10 of the obsolescent — but well liked — 'B12s' were authorised. But in view of the heavy weather Doncaster was making of the new design, matters were to an extent taken out of Gresley's hands, as Lord Faringdon, the LNER Deputy Chairman, entered directly into negotiations with Sir Hugh Reid, Chairman of the North British Locomotive Co (NBL). They had recently built 50 'Royal Scots' for the LMS — powerful three-cylinder 4-6-0s, although with an axle weight of 21¼ tons; the outline for these had been prepared at Derby, detailed design being shared with North British. The manufacturers agreed to a 'design and construct' contract for 10 of the new LNER locomotives, and work commenced immediately.

It is not known how much LNER design work was sent to NBL, although standard details were certainly passed on. From such evidence as is available, not only were the basics settled by the manufacturers but the design was worked up, and the drawings made, in their drawing office. The design of the boiler is of particular interest, as it might be thought that a taper boiler would have done something to ameliorate the weight problem, but at the time Gresley had only applied this to his largest engines, and in any case the urgency of the situation did not permit the lengthy delay which would ensue whilst this new concept was worked up. In the event a new parallel boiler was drawn out, which was little different from that fitted to the LNER 2-8-0s of the 'O1' and 'O2' classes — NBL having built 10 of the latter in 1921. The diameter was the same, at 5ft 6in, and the length of 14ft 0½in only 1½in less. The number of boiler tubes was reduced from 160 in the 2-8-0s to 143, the resultant improvement in water circulation being presumably held to more than offset the reduction in heating surface, but the flue and superheater arrangements remained the same. The firebox was a completely new design, with a grate area of 27.5sq ft. The boiler was in fact destined to play an important part in later LNER locomotive history.

Overall the outline was unmistakably that of Doncaster, the

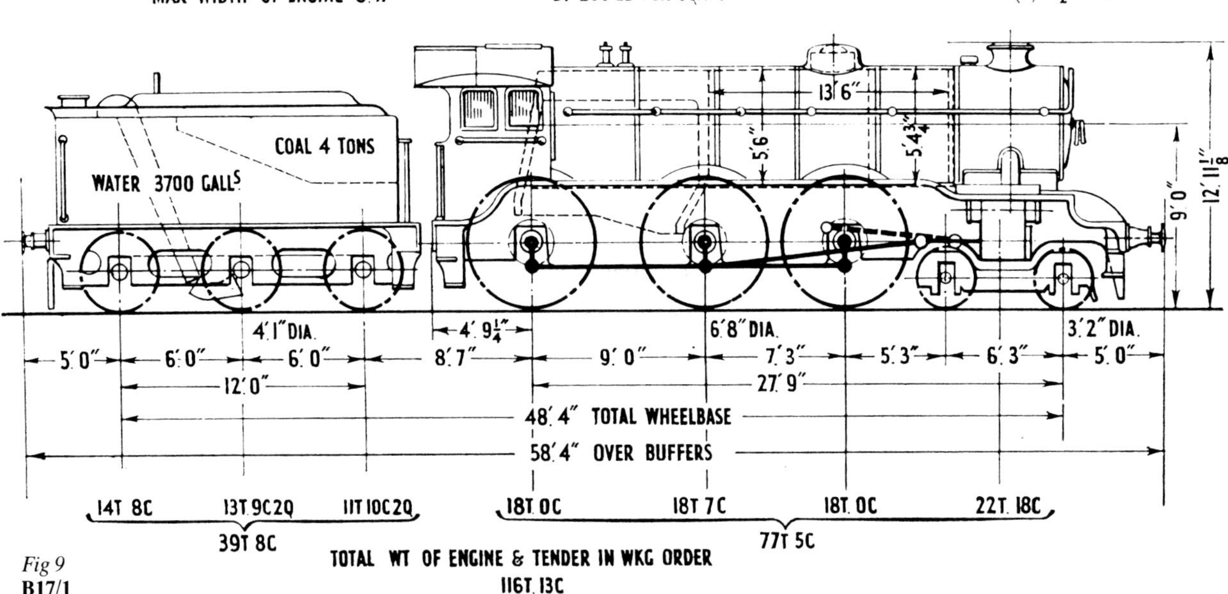

Fig 9
B17/1

soft 'S' curves of the footplating over the cylinders and beneath the cab contrasting with the sharper quadrants of the Darlington-designed 'Shires'. However, the smokebox door, with its short, widely spaced hinge straps, clearly owed its origins to Darlington. The cab followed that of the Pacifics, 20 of which had been built by NBL four years earlier. An advantage of the divided drive was that the forward positioning of the inside cylinder enabled the 2 to 1 gear for the inside valves to be fitted behind the cylinders, so keeping it free from the deposit of smokebox ash. This followed the method adopted for the 'Shires' and, incidentally, Gresley's first essay into derived valve gear, in his GNR 2-8-0 No 461.

The most important aspect of the new design was that it demonstrated the impossibility of Gresley's requirement that all three cylinders should drive on to the same coupled axle. To shift weight away from the driving axles and transfer it to the bogie, the position of the inside cylinder was moved forward and the drive made on to the leading axle, as on the 'Royal Scots'. In this form the weight distribution was such that the maximum axle load came out at 18 tons.

Surviving NBL records throw little light on the subject, although a note has been discovered which states 'We to draw out using Railway Company's standard details', confirming that the general arrangement was produced by the contractors, but with some assistance at least from the LNER. There is evidence that the boiler pressure was originally set at the usual Gresley figure of 180lb/sq in (at that time only the 'A3' Pacifics had a higher pressure), but to achieve the tractive effort called for, the pressure of the new engines was raised to 200lb/sq in. No radical design alteration was involved, but the firebox staying arrangements were no doubt strengthened. Also, it was realised that if the short Great Eastern pattern tender was employed, the firebox could be lengthened by 5in and the overall wheelbase could still be kept within the maximum permitted for turning on existing turntables.

The contract was finally confirmed on 17 February 1928, the quotation amounting to £7,280 for each of the 10 engines. NBL had up to then sought an order for 20 to justify this price, but Faringdon's authority only extended to 10, and in view of the poor state of their order book the contractors conceded the point. Delivery was promised in 30 to 38 weeks, so there was no expectation of any being delivered in time for the peak summer traffic; in fact, despite the delays caused by alterations, and the need to complete the drawings, the first engine was completed on 30 November and the last on 27 December.

It is not known to what extent NBL expected to build a larger number of engines, so that their design effort would be spread wider and hence the costs would be more likely to be recovered. Possibly the package was accepted not only to provide employment in the works but also to maintain continuity in the design office, as this was a capability which the company often used for the benefit of smaller overseas railways not possessing such resources of their own. In the event, the costings revealed a substantial loss on the contract, the locomotives working out at £8,514 each, leading to an overall loss of £12,340. The drawing office costs amounted to £4,040, contributing a third of this. However, NBL applied what was then a relatively high oncost to cover overheads — an average of 116% for example to workshop labour and materials — and it is probable that an element of profit was contained in this figure. In any case, their estimating tended to be on the low side: even the 50 LMS 'Royal Scots' showed an overall profit of only £20 per engine.

The 10 engines were identical except for one detail, the first five being fitted with Owen's patent regulator, and the remainder with NBL's own version. One regulator proved to be defective, a replacement being sent to Stratford in April 1929. As an example of the costs of accessories in those days, Ross pop safety valves were bought in for £8.25 per locomotive, whilst — as an extra — a pair of nameplates, designed, cast, finished and fitted, were charged to the LNER at 9 guineas a pair (£4.72½ each). There was evidently a misunderstanding at first over the positioning of the nameplates. The 'Royal Scots' had theirs on the leading splashers, as the Belpaire firebox permitted only a part splasher over the driving wheels, and NBL also positioned the names of the first four LNER engines over the leading splashers. This was soon corrected, although it is said that the first engine to be delivered had one plate over the leading splasher and the other over the middle one, the matter being corrected at Eastfield shed, Glasgow after delivery.

Whether the locomotives as completed by NBL were put on the scales to ascertain the accuracy of the calculated weights, or whether the LNER bothered to check these, is not known. There was undoubtedly a good deal of latitude in the Engineer's assessment of the maximum loads particular bridges would carry, and so long as he was assured by the CME that his strictures were observed, he would probably not take the matter further. For their part, neither the CME nor the Operating Superintendent would have looked further into the matter than they had to, being content with the manufacturer's figures. However, NBL were precise in their detailing of the difference between the tare weight of the engines, and the all-up weight ready for the road. Water in the boiler would account for an additional 6ton 2cwt, there would be 10cwt of coal in the firebox and 4cwt of sand in the sandboxes, whilst two men on the footplate would account for a further 3cwt — altogether, another 6ton 19cwt.

Whilst the engines were under construction, it was decided by the Chief General Manager that the practice of giving names to express passenger locomotives would be extended to the new class, and country estates, mainly in East Anglia, were selected for this purpose. The first of the class was named *Sandringham*, but this apart, the names chosen meant little to the travelling public. Unlike other new LNER classes, the running numbers commenced at a round hundred, the first being numbered 2800, and uniquely for a numerous LNER class, all, including those built later, bore consecutive numbers.

The new engines were far from trouble-free in the early years, and were sometimes criticised for poor steaming, but minor alterations to the draughting arrangements effected a cure. More seriously, the frames were prone to fracture, and all but one of the first 10 were given new frames within two years, the problem having been traced to excessive stiffness in the original design. Whilst the trouble was being diagnosed, and a cure worked out, several of the class were out of action for a period of months. However, the design was well proportioned and plenty of steam was available if the locomotive was properly fired. Despite the troubles associated with its initial construction, Gresley evidently looked on it with affection as one of his own — as, in its broad specification, it certainly was. A continuing drawback, common to all his tender engines other than those with a trailing axle, was the hard riding, particularly of high mileage engines, and which no adjustment of springs or axlebox wedges seemed to cure. On the other hand, the placing of the 2 to 1 gear behind the cylinders gave rise to less wear in the linkages, and the 'B17s' did not get out of adjustment to the same extent as other Gresley three-cylinder classes.

Continuing pressure for additional locomotive power from the Great Eastern section operating department resulted in authorisation of a further 12 by the LNER Board on 29 November 1928, as part of the 1929 locomotive building programme, even before the first had been delivered from NBL. Despite protestations by the manufacturers, who not unreasonably looked for another order to help offset the losses sustained in building the first batch, the work was given to the LNER shops at Darlington. To add insult to injury, the boilers were contracted out to Armstrong Whitworth, who quoted £1,388 for each boiler against the NBL price of £1,430. The Darlington estimate of the total cost was £6,600 per engine.

The following November, despite the troubles which had beset the initial batch, the Chief General Manager was able to report to the Board that the class had proved very satisfactory, and 15 more were included in the 1930 Programme, five to replace 'B12s' transferred to the Northern Scottish Area, and 10 in place of old 'D13' 4-4-0s which were to be withdrawn. By the time these had been delivered — again, built at Darlington — any initially unfavourable reception by Great Eastern enginemen had been overcome. After all, this was not unreasonable: the 'B17s' represented a radically different attitude to locomotive design to that of the simple two-cylinder classes to which the crews were accustomed. Once the draughting problem had been overcome, the locomotives gained a reputation for free steaming, and the higher tractive effort was welcomed, as was the left-hand drive. Six more were turned out from Darlington in 1933, and a further five in 1935, all with detailed amendments to the original design, including alterations to the springing arrangements in efforts to improve the riding. The estimated cost had now come down to £6,300 per locomotive, no doubt reflecting the ability of the workshops to improve productivity when building to a standard design. However, an interesting

Below:
The 'East Anglian' did not run at weekends, leaving the pair of streamlined 'B17/5s' free for other duties. At March, in August 1938, No 2859 waits to work forward on the 3.53pm (SO) Liverpool-Yarmouth express. *Eric Neve*

Above:
No 2806 *Audley End*, named after the country house near Saffron Walden, is seen in charge of a stopping train to Felixstowe, c1932. The location is Romford, with the LMS branch from Upminster on the extreme left. *Real Photos (R1695)*

commentary on an apparent lack of detailed supervision was the provision of side chains on the tender drawbar. These, intended as a back-up should the coupling hook become broken, had long been discarded in practice, but remained on the outdated drawing from which the GER pattern tenders were constructed, and consequently were fitted to all 48 built thus far.

A new development took place in 1936 when 14 'B17s' were built, also at Darlington, specially for service on the Great Central section. Since the restrictions on overall length did not apply, the short GE tender was replaced by the LNER 4,200gal group standard type. By now the Darlington estimate had fallen still further to £6,000 per engine, although it is possible that the higher cost of the larger tender had not been taken into consideration. A most interesting innovation was introduced with this batch in that they received names, not of country estates, but of football clubs, the first being No 2848, *Arsenal*.

The Government's New Works Programme of 1935 provided the LNER with a low cost loan of nearly £6 million, of which the largest single appropriation was £2.6 million for the electrification of the Manchester, Sheffield and Wath line. £288,500 was allocated to new locomotives, these being 17 'A4s', five 'V2s', 10 'K3s' and 11 more 'B17s', some of which were to replace Great Eastern 'B12s' to be sent to Aberdeen, so permitting the withdrawal of elderly Great North of Scotland 4-4-0s. As Doncaster were to build the 'A4s' and Darlington were to be engaged on a long production run of 'V2s', it was decided to put the 'K3s' and the 'B17s' out to contract; in any case, the Government had wanted to see orders placed with the private builders. The successful tenderers for the 4-6-0s were Robert Stephenson & Co Ltd, the price being £6,960 for each engine — substantially higher than the figure last quoted by Darlington. The price might have been even higher but, under pressure from the CME, Stephenson reduced their quotation by £500 per engine. Five other manufacturers, including NBL, submitted unsuccessful tenders. The locomotives were all delivered during the first seven months of 1937, a delay having ensued as a result of Stephenson having lost skilled men to the armaments industry, and having suffered a strike by those who remained, who sought higher wages to match those then being paid by such firms as Vickers, who were busy on Government rearmament contracts.

These were the last of the class to be built, although a further 32 were included in the 1937 Building Programme, first discussed in October 1936, which also included 11 of the newly introduced 'V2s'. However, Sir Nigel Gresley was evidently having further thoughts about the limited capability of the 'B17s', as he qualified the statements in the programme by saying that he contemplated the substitution of an 'improved type of engine' in place of the 'B17s'. A month later he had made his mind up, concluding that a further new type was not justified, and that whereas a more powerful class than the 'B17' was needed for sections other than the Great Eastern, the 'V2' would meet these requirements. For the same price as the 32 'B17s', 28 of these 2-6-2s could be built, and this was how the matter was left.

Details of the 'improved type of engine' were revealed in March 1947, when Gresley's technical assistant Bert Spencer read a paper before the Institution of Locomotive Engineers entitled 'The Development of LNER Locomotive Design 1923-1941'. (E. S. Cox had previously read a Paper in which he described a number of LMS 'might-have-beens', and it is thought that this stimulated Arthur Peppercorn, then CME of the LNER, into putting up Spencer to give similar information about unfulfilled Gresley projects, in a wide-ranging survey of LNER locomotive practice.) Spencer had been brought to King's Cross from Doncaster drawing office around the time of the Grouping and was in a unique position to describe the evolution of Gresley's designs. He described the proposed locomotive as a large 4-6-0 comparable with the Great Western 'Castle' class, with a taper boiler pressured to 220lb/sq in and a tractive effort of 31,200lb — an increase of nearly a quarter over that of the 'B17s', and not far short of the 33,730lb of the 'V2s'. There is no evidence that this proposal ever progressed beyond an outline drawing, but the inference is that Gresley, breaking new ground in his high powered 2-6-2, wanted to be assured of its ability to haul fast passenger trains in safety before embarking on a programme of construction in which substantial numbers would be engaged on these services. Reservations had been expressed about the widespread use of the 'V2', which had been originally

Right:
The first 'Sandringham' to be seen at King's Cross was No 2819 *Welbeck Abbey*, having worked up one day in 1930 from Cambridge, where it was stationed for almost all its career. Here it is seen on a summer afternoon in 1934 at Whittlesford with a heavy down Cambridge line express. The train engine is 'D15/2' No 8797.
Real Photos (23861)

intended as an improvement on the 'K3' 2-6-0 for fast goods traffic, but with its 6ft 2in wheels giving it a higher turn of speed, and its large boiler and wide firebox providing the capability for the sustained high power output needed to work heavy long distance passenger trains. There were anxieties about the use of a leading pony truck instead of a bogie, as well as over the weight and length of the 'V2s', which would restrict their route availability. Consequently, the large 4-6-0 was outlined as a hedge against the 'V2' turning out to be unsuitable for a wide ranging mixed traffic role, and therefore having to be supplemented by a 4-6-0 for the faster passenger services, as a back-up to the Pacifics. However, it was not long before the 'V2' was seen to be all that its designer had expected, and the need for the new 4-6-0 disappeared, although with 22 tons on its driving axles it would have been prohibited from the Great Eastern section anyway.

Two important developments in the 'B17' design took place under Edward Thompson. The most fundamental was the complete rebuilding of 10 members of the class with two cylinders, as described in the next chapter, but also of importance was the re-equipment of most of the remainder with 225lb boilers. This increased the nominal tractive effort to 28,553lb, which should have given a welcome boost to their capability. However, nothing seems to have been recorded of any special performances by any of the rebuilds, which were classified 'B17/6'.

Following the introduction of the streamlined trains, a new express, titled the 'East Anglian' was introduced to the Great Eastern section. This ran up from Norwich at 11.55am, reaching Liverpool Street at 2.10pm, and returning at 6.40pm — a 4min stop being made at Ipswich in each direction. However, congestion on the GE main line which was only double track throughout almost its entire length, as well as the difficult nature of the road, precluded anything like the speeds which were scheduled on the East Coast main line, the highest start-to-stop speed being 54.5mph between Ipswich and Norwich. However, 3min were cut from the running time in the following year, raising the average speed over this section to 57.9mph. New stock was provided, but with standard teak panelling, unlike the smoothed exterior of the three King's Cross trains, although the feature of serving meals at all seats was maintained. The 'East Anglian' was made up of only six coaches, but the furnishings provided a much higher standard of comfort than the standard stock, and the total weight was 220 tons tare. To take advantage of the streamline vogue, two of the 'B17s' were given an overall sheet metal covering similar to that of the 'A4s', but ran in green livery, not being accorded the blue of the Pacifics. The two engines, No 2859 *East Anglian* and No 2870 *City of London* were both stationed at Norwich, where the train originated. They were reclassified 'B17/5'.

The first part of the LNER system to see the 'B17s' in action was the Southern Scottish Area; delivery of the initial batch was made from NBL to Cowlairs Works, and after acceptance they were run in one at a time on the NB main line between Glasgow and Edinburgh, and indeed as far as Dundee, thus being the first 4-6-0s to run on these routes. However, they did not stay in Scotland for any length of time, and before long were seen at work in England. Cecil J. Allen was not long in sampling the performance of the new engines, and in his monthly article in the *Railway Magazine* of April 1929 reported two trips he had made behind members of the class working the eastbound 'North Country Continental' between Manchester and Sheffield. With no more than 240 tons behind the tender, both engines lost time, even after making allowances for signal and other delays, and Allen described their performance as disappointing. This was in sharp contrast to that of a Great Northern Atlantic working a Great Central section express westwards over the same route, which gained time with a similar load. However, he reported that the engines were doing excellent work on the Great Eastern, particularly on the Parkeston Quay boat trains. In an early run behind No 2803 *Framlingham* hauling a 460-ton 'Hook Continental' on an 87min schedule, two serious signal checks were suffered, but Allen computed the net time to be no more than 84min. With the somewhat lighter 'Flushing Continental', although still grossing some 360 tons, the 85min schedule was cut despite permanent way and signal checks en route. A notable feature was the ability of the engine to accelerate, especially from the 20mph slack for the Manningtree curve, but the combination of a heavy load and a difficult road precluded very high speeds, a little over 70mph being the best recorded. In fact, despite their unspectacular start, the 'B17s' were the only examples of their type in Britain which could exert 1,500ihp and at the same time be acceptable to the GE Section Civil Engineer.

The fastest speeds sustained by 'B17s' on the Great Eastern were probably achieved by the two locomotives engaged on the 'East Anglian', which often demonstrated their ability to run the 116 miles between Liverpool Street and Norwich in even time, neglecting the standing time at Ipswich. Generally speaking, a much clearer road was obtained between Ipswich and Norwich, enabling high speeds to be maintained such as, on one occasion, 74mph with No 2870 over the severely undulating 38.4 miles between Claydon and MP 112. Maximum speeds recorded were 85mph near Flordon, 82mph at Diss, and even 80mph through Witham in the first half of the journey. However, the 'East Anglian' schedule demanded only modest power output compared with the heavier, albeit slower, trains.

Although the 'B17s' were originally built for East Anglia, many of the class performed useful service on the Great Central in the 1930s. Their first posting was to Gorton, to take over from the 'B12s' in hauling the 'North Country Continental' on its long journey to and from the Essex coast. By 1931, Gorton had two 'B17s' for this work, the spare engine being used on fill-in turns to Sheffield and Leicester. Two years later, Gorton's allocation had been increased to six, and regular workings commenced on the London Extension, primarily on a daily lodging turn. Neasden received three in 1935, but 'B17s' did not work a majority of services to London until the following year, when six 'Footballers' were delivered new to Leicester shed, replacing the 'C4' Atlantics, and for a couple of years the class were generally the first choice for most services between Marylebone, Sheffield and Manchester. However, in 1938, 'A1' Pacifics were becoming surplus to requirements on the East Coast main line as a result of new 'A4s' coming into service and numbers of 'V2s' were built for allocation to the Great Central section. The influx of these larger engines resulted in the transfer away of the 'B17s', although a few returned to Gorton during the war. Later, a number found their way on to Great Central metals from Colwick, where no fewer than nine were stationed at the time of Nationalisation, but it was not many years before all were concentrated in East Anglia.

During the short period when the 'B17s' could be seen at Marylebone, many excellent runs were recorded. Their first regular appearances on the London Extension included working the 2.32am newspaper flyer, which at the time of the Grouping held the position (jointly with the North Eastern) of being the fastest train in Britain. This sprang from the 61.4mph of the schedule between Leicester and Nottingham Arkwright Street, in the early hours of the morning. O. S. Nock gave up a night's sleep to record a trip on this train, headed on this occasion by No 2841 *Gayton Hall*. With nine bogies totalling 300 tons (although weighing less after each stop, as newspapers were offloaded) the locomotive was driven on full regulator and short cut-offs wherever possible, and pared 1¼min from the 66min schedule over the 59.3 miles from Marylebone to Brackley, averaging 54.9mph. The engine did even better on to Rugby, averaging 60.4mph start-to-stop over the 23.9 miles, for which the schedule was 25½min; 50mph was sustained up the long 1 in 176 out of Brackley, and 85mph was achieved at Braunston.

A train which was frequently in the hands of the 'Footballers' was the 6.20pm down from Marylebone, which took the GW/GC joint line via High Wycombe, 66min being allowed for the first stage of 59 miles to Finmere. A run behind No 2849 *Sheffield United* with nine coaches totalling 325 tons resulted in a cut of 2½min from the schedule. In the mid-1930s it became the practice to add extra vehicles to the 6.20pm down, to cater for returning day excursion passengers, and because of this No 2849 *Sheffield United* had to tackle 11 bogies weighing 400 tons, which it ran to Leicester in a net time of 1min less than the schedule. On another occasion, an exceptionally heavy train grossing 475 tons was headed by *two* 'B17s', No 2855 *Middlesbrough* and No 2842 *Kilverstone Hall*. After suffering two signal checks, 4min were lost to Finmere, but were all but regained by the time Leicester was reached, the 34 miles from Woodford being run at an average of 65mph, with a maximum speed of no less than 92mph at Whetstone.

'B17s' were seen at King's Cross from 1930, as a number were kept at Cambridge for working trains to London, including, after 1932, the well known buffet car expresses, although it was many years before they replaced Ivatt Atlantics as the regular engines on these services. After Nationalisation, the entire class was stationed in East Anglia, with a heavy concentration at Cambridge, and they were then seen several times a day at King's Cross.

Although all but the first ten were built in the North-East, the class did not receive a welcome in that Area, none being permanently based there. Batches of 'B17s' were twice proposed for the North-Eastern Area in the initial discussion leading up to preparation of the annual locomotive programme, but on each occasion mixed traffic locomotives were preferred — 'K3s' in the 1934 programme, and 'V2s' in that for 1937. This does not mean however that 'B17s' were not seen in the northeast, as newly built engines were used on running-in turns, and they were sometimes noticed on visiting excursions — usually in connection with soccer matches. In 1937, a through working was in existence for a period from Leicester to Newcastle, and a Sheffield 'B17' worked into Hull Paragon with a train from Liverpool. An interesting extramural activity in 1937 was the working by a Sheffield-based 'Footballer' over GWR metals between Banbury, Oxford and Swindon, and return. No 2863 *Everton* is on record as having beaten the 'Cheltenham Flyer' schedule between Swindon and Foxhall Junction, Didcot, a top speed of 88mph being achieved at Wantage Road.

The naming of the 'B17s' is an interesting study, there being four groups of names, plus one singleton. The original

Left:
The last two of the 1935 batch of 'B17s' built at Darlington were sent to March to replace 'Immingham' 4-6-0s on passenger duties centred there. No 2847 *Helmingham Hall* was at March for three years before being reallocated to Woodford. It is seen in August 1938 at Peterborough North, just before its transfer, with the empty stock of the 3.20pm stopping train to March and Ely. The use of these modern locomotives on such secondary duties seems to indicate a preference for 'B12/3s' on many Great Eastern services.
Eric Neve

Right:
The chime whistle is blowing as streamlined 'B17/5' 4-6-0 No 1670 *City of London* hustles an up express past Bentley Junction box, south of Ipswich, on 23 August 1947. The engine is still in wartime black livery, the valances over the coupled wheels having been removed in 1942. *G. R. Mortimer*

'Sandringham' theme was continued until 48 locomotives bore the names of country estates, four being named after the seats of LNER Directors. The press release announcing the arrival of the first of the class said that it was named by 'kind permission of His Majesty', and one presumes that the permission of other owners was also sought beforehand. If so, this makes the choice of *Rendelsham Hall* for No 2839 seem a little strange, as not only was the name spelled incorrectly, but the building was in use as a nursing home. No 2847 *Helmingham Hall* (in Suffolk, and well away from Great Western territory) shared the name with GWR Hall No 6947.

The second series were the 'Footballers', commencing with No 2848 *Arsenal*, the first of 25 originally given the names of leading football clubs whose grounds were serviced by the LNER. (An omission which may surprise present-day fans was *Ipswich Town*, but the fact is that the club was not elected to the Football League until the 1938-39 season.) The intention was of course to use the appropriate engine to haul supporters' specials, but this was not always possible, particularly if the engine in question was undergoing repair at the time it was needed, and consequently there were a number of temporary transfers of identity to ensure that fans were not disappointed by the non-availability of 'their' engine. Conversely, no cases are on record of a 'Footballer' being attacked by supporters of a rival club.

The other two groups of names were smaller and mostly resulted from renaming. Two of the 'Footballers', Nos 2859 and 2870 became *East Anglian* and *City of London* respectively, when selected for streamlining and working the 'East Anglian', and three others were given regimental names; No 2858 *Newcastle United* became *The Essex Regiment* only days after it had entered service — not unreasonably, perhaps, since the locomotive was not stationed in Newcastle, but at Parkeston; the others were No 2805 *Lincolnshire Regiment* (originally *Burnham Thorpe*) and No 2845 *The Suffolk Regiment*. Finally, No 2871 the first to be rebuilt as a 'B2' (see Chapter 6) was renamed *Royal Sovereign* and stationed at Cambridge, specially to work the Royal trains between King's Cross and King's Lynn in place of the 'Royal Clauds' which had previously carried out this duty.

The longest-lived 'B17' was No 2808 *Gunton* which was withdrawn early in 1960 after almost 31 years of service, having accumulated around a million miles, mostly when based at Stratford. In fact, a majority of the original 10, including No 2800 *Sandringham* itself, lasted for 30 years. Four were withdrawn in 1952-53, but otherwise most kept going until the end of the 1950s, the last to disappear being No 2868 *Bradford City* in August 1960. The introduction of the 'Britannias' in 1951 led to relegation of the 'B17s' into the background of East Anglian workings, but even so there were occasions when one had to deputise for a Pacific in an emergency. However, they became increasingly used on lesser duties, those with the short GE tender being valued for branch and cross-country services on which the larger engines could not be accommodated on the turntables, because of their length, or for reasons of weight.

Right:
One of the first batch of 'Footballers', No 2854 *Sunderland*, went new to Leicester shed, and shortly afterwards is seen leaving Marylebone with the 5.00pm to Nottingham on 23 May 1936. As well as the representation of a football, the centre splashers were adorned with the club colours, in this case red and white stripes.
LCGB/Ken Nunn Collection

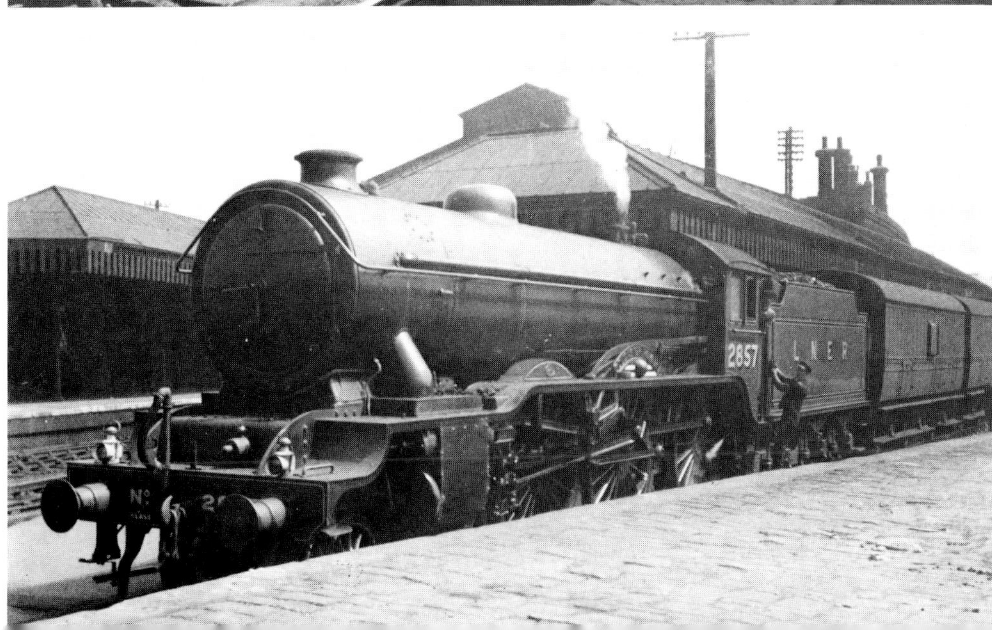

Left:
'B17s' on diverse Pullman workings. (Left) No 2872 *West Ham United* recently delivered from Robert Stephenson's works at Darlington, is seen working the down 'Queen of Scots' between Eryholme and Croft Spa on 31 July 1937. Shortly afterwards it was transferred to Norwich, and distinguished itself in April 1938 by working the 'East Anglian' when both the streamlined 'B17s' were stopped for repairs. (Lower left) No 2835 *Milton* heads the down 'Eastern Belle' passing Chadwell Heath on its way to Cromer in 1938. This locomotive had also been moved to Norwich after several years at Doncaster, from which depot it worked fish trains originating at Hull.
J. F. Aylard; Real Photos (23867)

Below left:
No 2834 *Hinchingbrooke* and 'B3' No 6169 *Lord Faringdon* at Sheffield Victoria, both in pristine condition and making a splendid sight. No 2834 was one of the 'B17s' with the longest service on the Great Central section, most of its time between 1931 and 1939 being spent at Gorton. The two engines are standing in the 'middle siding', probably waiting to take over trains arriving from the Manchester direction.
Stephenson Locomotive Society

Bottom left:
'Footballer' No 2857 *Doncaster Rovers* is in charge of empty stock at Sheffield Victoria in 1939. This was one of the group of engines allocated to Neasden for general work on the London Extension. Later it moved to Colwick before being transferred to East Anglia, where all the 'B17s' were eventually stationed. It was never allocated to Doncaster shed.
Hughes Junction

2844
L N E R

L N E R
2833

Nº 61619

Left:
An open day was held at North Road, Darlington, on 5-6 May 1935. Amongst the engines on display was No 2844, *Earlham Hall*, newly turned out from Darlington Works. (Note the green-painted cylinders, a characteristic of Darlington. In the absence of a precise all-line painting specification, these were painted black elsewhere.) Earlham Hall itself was situated near Norwich, and in a rare instance of local posting, No 2844 was allocated to Norwich until it was rebuilt as a 'B2' in 1949.
Ian N. Fraser

Centre left:
'B17s' were sometimes seen south of Hitchin in prewar days, generally on a Cambridge working. However, No 2833 *Kimbolton Castle* was one of three allocated to Doncaster from new, their primary duty being to work fish trains from Hull to Doncaster and on to Banbury. At the weekends, the engines were available for other jobs, and No 2833 is seen near Brookmans Park in 1937 heading an excursion train to King's Cross.
Kenneth Leech/Colour-Rail

Bottom left:
Borrowed by King's Cross for a fill-in outer suburban turn, No 61619 *Welbeck Abbey* is approaching New Southgate soon after Nationalisation. The new number is painted on the cabside in shaded LNER block numerals, and other interesting details are the combination of headcode disc and lamp on the same lamp-iron, and the unusually tall vacuum standpipe.
Wethersett Collection/Ian Allan Library

Above right:
No 61657 *Doncaster Rovers* is on FA cup duty waiting to take its team's supporters to Middlesbrough for a fourth round tie on 6 February 1952. The engine has been rebuilt with a 100A boiler and reclassified 'B17/6'. The result of the match was a 4-1 win for Doncaster, but they were knocked out in a later round. The cup was won by Newcastle United, for whom the immortal Jackie Milburn scored one of their goals. *Geoffrey Oates*

Right:
On 19 February 1949, No 61634 *Hinchingbrooke*, in early British Railways livery, is working hard with an up special approaching Bentley. A cold morning adds sharpness to the appearance of the engine's exhaust. *G. R. Mortimer*

6

Thompson 4-6-0s

Sir Nigel Gresley sadly passed away on 5 April 1941; he had not been in good health for some time, but was within two months of his 65th birthday, when he would have retired in accordance with LNER policy. However, the LNER Board had made no provision for a successor, and since Gresley himself had made no mention of retiring, it is likely that in the circumstances of World War 2 he would have continued in office, at least for the time being. No post of Deputy Chief Mechanical Engineer existed, and his principal Head Office assistant, D. R. Edge, was limited in experience and had been primarily concerned with the administration of the Department. It has been said that Sir Ronald Matthews, the LNER Chairman, approached Sir Herbert Walker to see if Oliver Bulleid might be attracted back to the LNER, and also enquired about the availability of Roland Bond of the LMS, who had been placed in charge of the Locomotive Testing Station at Rugby, which was being constructed as a joint enterprise by the LNER and the LMS. Not meeting with success in either of these overtures, the Board decided to give the appointment to Edward Thompson, who had occupied the position of Mechanical Engineer, Southern Area (Western) at Doncaster since the retirement of R. A. Thom in June 1938. Previously, Thompson had been in the similar post at Darlington, and before that he was at Stratford; he had had wide experience of the workshops, and was well qualified technically for the job of Chief Mechanical Engineer. He was reputed however, to have been of a taciturn nature, and not always on the best terms with his staff.

Thompson has been said to have been critical of certain aspects of Gresley's locomotive style, but he had been instrumental in the modernisation of the Great Eastern 'Claud Hamilton' 4-4-0s, and 'B12' 4-6-0s, whilst later at Darlington he had begun similar work on the 'D20' 4-4-0s. He had been given successive promotions by Gresley, and although it has often been said that their personalities were poles apart, this would not necessarily detract from his ability as an engineering manager.

At his appointment, Thompson was only five years short of retiring age, so that had Gresley continued in post it would have been increasingly unlikely that the CME's job would have gone to him; as it was, he had only a relatively short period in office, and, taking over in the middle of a war, the prospects for his earning a name for himself as a worthy successor to Sir Nigel Gresley were limited. Wartime stresses were heavy, and Thompson had more urgent matters than long term locomotive strategy with which to occupy himself. The priority at the time was to keep the rolling stock, and particularly the locomotives, in running order to cope with the massive demands made upon them, the task being rendered all the more onerous by the diversion of much of the workshop capability to the manufacture of war material.

Thompson was aware of the difficulties, aggravated in wartime, of maintaining in good condition the Gresley '2 to 1' drive for the valves of the centre cylinder of three-cylinder engines. Perhaps reports of failures due to this component, or of poor locomotive performance resulting from it, were exaggerated as there is plenty of evidence of first class work by the Gresley fleet of big engines in the early 1940s; but Thompson concluded that the conjugated gear was a source of weakness unless it was maintained in good order, and his new appointment enabled him to crystallise his ideas and put them into practice.

His first move was to obtain an independent view on the efficacy of the '2 to 1' gear, and for this he approached W. A. Stanier, CME of the LMS, who arranged for his Chief Technical Assistant, E. S. Cox, to visit Doncaster to examine the situation. In a full and well argued report, Cox acknowledged that the gear was theoretically correct, but that wear in the linkage to the centre cylinder led to considerable inequality of output between the outside and centre cylinders — so much so that at high speeds the centre cylinder could develop considerably more power than either of the outside cylinders, this in turn placing excessive stress on the middle big end. Together with an internally obtained, and possibly selective, report on breakdowns on the road due to failures of the Gresley gear, this was sufficient to give Thompson the evidence he needed to convince his Board that a reversal of Gresley's three-cylinder policy was warranted.

Thompson's Memorandum to the LNER Board — submitted as was usual in the name of the Chief General Manager, Sir Charles Newton — was convincing and timely. His main proposals were for the conversion of one of the 2-8-2 'P2s' to the 4-6-2 wheel arrangement, cessation of further construction of 'V2' locomotives, and the construction of 10 locomotives of a two-cylinder 4-6-0 type, 'entirely composed of existing standard

Above right:
Robert Urie initiated a new design of 4-6-0 mixed traffic locomotive for the London & South Western Railway in 1914, known as the 'H15' class. Important features were a high running plate almost completely exposing the coupled wheels, and outside Walschaerts valve gear. This was in complete contrast to the then British convention of placing as much of the machinery as possible between the frames, and providing much lower running plates, with large splashers. A second batch of 'H15s', somewhat modified, was built by the Southern Railway at Eastleigh in 1924, one of which was No E476. *Real Photos*

Right:
Edward Thompson's 'B1' class came out in 1942, differing in almost every detail with the Urie design, but substantially the same in concept. No 61059 was built by NBL in 1946, and was one of seven sent new to Ipswich shed. Originally turned out in black with red lining and shaded block characters, it never bore LNER green, and is seen at Stratford in British Railways lined black on 2 September 1951. For once, it was not in its normal state of cleanliness, the reason being that it was shortly to enter the workshops. On completion of its overhaul, in the hands of Drivers Calver and Cocksedge, it became the 'Pride of Ipswich'.
E. D. Bruton

parts, which will be roughly equivalent to the existing "K3" class, but of simpler design'. The proposals were accepted by the Board, the first two leading to the much criticised rebuilding of the 'Cock o' the North' class and later to Thompson's somewhat ungainly Pacifics, but the third resulted in what was to be his *chef-d'oeuvre*, the 'B1' 4-6-0, of which 410 were built, numerically by far the largest class to be constructed to a LNER design.

Thompson no doubt had in mind the Great Western 'Halls' and the LMS 'Black Fives' when conceiving his medium power mixed traffic locomotive. In effect he introduced the LNER equivalent of these two very successful classes, particularly the latter, which was a fitter's dream, with all its machinery outside the frames. Robert Urie of the London & South Western Railway had also produced a very similar engine over 25 years before, known as the 'H15' class, but it is unlikely that Thompson took this as his model. Nevertheless, many of its main features were followed. The new 4-6-0 had as its boiler a modified version of that fitted to the Gresley 'B17' class, some minor strengthening being needed to permit an increase of boiler pressure to 225lb/sq in. (This development had in fact been conceived in outline in 1939, but no detailed work was put in hand until Thompson decided to proceed with his new 4-6-0.) The two outside cylinders were similar to those fitted many years earlier to Gresley's 'K2' Moguls, although new patterns had to be made as Thompson kept to the later Gresley type of three-bar slidebar in preference to the more cumbersome two-bar type used on the 2-6-0s. In the years since the report of the Bridge Stress Committee, attitudes had altered somewhat on the question of the balancing necessary to counteract the effects of hammerblow, so that Thompson was able to use two cylinders but still have the same route availability as the 'B17s'; originally, 36% of the reciprocating weights were balanced, this being later increased to 40%. The coupled wheels and cab followed those of the 'V2s', but the bogie design was new, with spring side control, replacing the Gresley swing link pattern. Nevertheless, by and large, Thompson's claim that he would develop the locomotive from existing standard parts was achieved. The draughtsman at Doncaster responsible for the drawings of the engine was Ted Parker.

The first of these new 4-6-0s, originally referred to as the 'B' class, but later given the classification 'B1', emerged from Darlington in December 1942 and was greeted with approbation from all sides. Its designer had contrived to produce a locomotive in the classic lines of the best British traditions, neat in outline yet with the appearance of power at hand. Clearly of LNER ancestry, it nevertheless lacked the softness of the Gresley outline, Thompson managing to implant certain new features which were to become a recognisable trademark of his own locomotives. The outside cylinders were noticeably larger in diameter than those of most of Gresley's three-cylinder designs, and to accommodate the cylinder casting, the running plate was raised to clear the driving wheels, following a straight line from smokebox to cab. A prominent quadrant in the Darlington style brought the running plate down to buffer beam level at the front end, but that beneath the cab was shortened, resulting in an

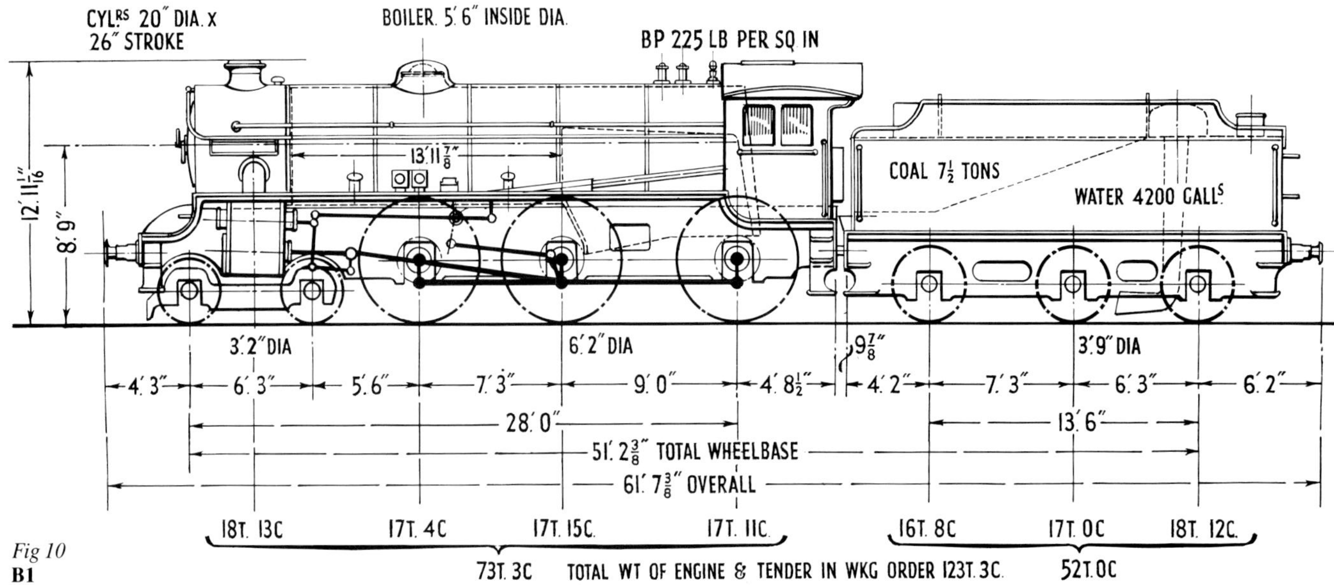

Fig 10
B1

Above:
The often workaday appearance of the 'B1s' is illustrated by No 61016 *Inyala* outside Mold motive power depot in April 1964. This engine led an uneventful life, spending its first 10 years at York. In 1963 it found its way to the Lancashire & Yorkshire shed at Mirfield and finished its days at Low Moor. The Inyala is a species of antelope found in Southern Africa, but it is doubtful whether this name meant very much to the passenger. *Ian Allan Library*

asymmetric outline. This has been criticised as spoiling an otherwise satisfactory appearance, particularly as the lower end of the cabside was several inches above that of the tender, but no doubt a worthwhile saving in weight of sheet steel was made in each engine — a total of several tons in all. (A minor alteration carried out at Cowlairs in BR days was the insertion of a fillet in the top angle of the forward quadrant, this being done to avoid cracking at this point.) The boiler mountings were of conventional Doncaster pattern, similar to those fitted to Gresley's 2-8-0s, and slightly higher than those of the 'B17s', the boiler of which was pitched 3in higher.

One important feature on which Thompson agreed with Gresley was the design of firebox, preferring the simpler round-top type to the more expensive Belpaire. The merits and demerits of each have never been satisfactorily evaluated, and decisions on which to use have depended on the personal choice of the engineer concerned. Doncaster practice had always favoured the round-top type, and not until the Stanier 2-8-0s were under construction in 1943-45 was the plant required to fabricate fireboxes in the unfamiliar Belpaire style. It is said that the Works Manager at the time, F. H. Eggleshaw, let it be known that an equivalent round-topped boiler would have reduced the cost considerably. This seems to be true, if only a small number were to be made to a particular pattern, but there was little difference in cost once the flanged plates had been produced. These must be made in a hydraulic press, using specially prepared blocks, whereas a skilled boilersmith could make those for the round-topped variety by hand. The original intention was to construct the 2-8-0s at Crewe, but under a change of plan the material was switched to Doncaster, and the probability is that the fireboxes were constructed there, with Crewe supplying the flanging blocks.

The main advantage claimed for the Belpaire is better steam generation, as more firebox heating surface is in contact with water, and more space is available above the firebox for water and steam; but against this its opponents hold that the first cost is excessive and greater maintenance is required. Gresley's preference is clear, as he not only built all his new engines with round-topped boxes, but rebuilt a number of pre-Grouping Belpaire classes. In contrast, a majority of post-Grouping engines on other railways were fitted with Belpaire boxes, the LMS and Great Western adopting this type, as well as the BR design team.

Noting Gresley's preference, it is a little strange to learn that his then newly appointed Technical Assistant, Bert Spencer, is on record as remarking on the benefits supposedly conferred by the Belpaire type, at a meeting of the Institution of Locomotive Engineers at Leeds in 1923. It is worth quoting his words verbatim:

'In view of its straightforward construction it is surprising that the Belpaire type of firebox has not been used to a greater extent in this country. The design provides a large steam space, and enables heavy girder stays to be dispensed with. Also, the large flat crown plate takes the effect of expansion much more easily than the more rigid round-topped box, and roof stay troubles are consequently reduced. The girder stays in use with round-topped fireboxes are not a highly satisfactory arrangement as immediately the boiler is heated the uneven expansion of the copper box in relation to the steel wrapper leaves the front part of the inner box unsupported.'

Gresley did not take part in the discussion — indeed it is unlikely that he was present — but Spencer was supported by G. A. Musgrave, speaking from his experience in locomotive workshops. (Some years afterwards he was to manage the workshops at Cowlairs, and later became Locomotive Running Superintendent in Scotland.) Musgrave stated that two flat surfaces, as in the Belpaire firebox, are more simply stayed than if one is flat and one is round. On the other hand, J. F. Harrison, who many years later was responsible for the design of the postwar 'A1' Pacifics, holds the view that circular-section vessels are cheaper to manufacture than those with square sides, and when under pressure tend to hold their shape, whilst others tend to become distorted. Thus maintenance of a round-topped boiler should be cheaper than of one of Belpaire type, particularly since the former has the ability to flex without the crown stays becoming broken. Conversely, Harrison has also pointed out that in good water areas the advantage of a large steam space with a small increase in maintenance costs outweighs the benefit of cheaper manufacture. However, in hard water areas, notably in the Great Central area — the worst in Britain — where firebox life could be as low as three or four years, when compared with perhaps 40 years in Scotland, the shed repairs on round-topped fireboxes were less, which added to lower maintenance costs gave the latter a decided advantage.

Another basic consideration for this class of locomotive was whether the boiler barrel should be parallel or tapered. Thompson's contemporaries in the Great Western and LMS had followed the latter pattern, as had Gresley on his largest engines, and his last steam design, the 'V4' 2-6-2, which in many ways was intended for similar duties to those set out for the 'B1' 4-6-0. The argument for tapering rests on the fact that the gases produced by the fire become cooler as they move further away from the firebox, therefore the boiler should be reduced in diameter towards its front in order to concentrate the heat. However, it is more costly to construct a tapered boiler than one which is parallel and the additional expense of such tapering may only be worthwhile in a large engine likely to be working hard for long periods at a stretch. It would be a matter of judgement whether a tapered boiler would add appreciably to the efficiency of a medium-sized general purpose engine which would be spending much of its time on duties not requiring a high level of steam generation. Another factor in the choice of a tapered boiler is the saving of weight at the front end, offsetting the additional weight of a Belpaire firebox should this be decided upon.

Thompson was evidently not impressed by the arguments in favour of tapering, and in any case he was in the middle of a war and had the Diagram 100 boiler of the 'B17s' ready to hand, which only needed a minimum of alteration to adapt it to his new engine. The most important change was the strengthening of the boiler plates from ⅝in to 11⁄16in thickness, to cope with an increase in the steam pressure. The amended design was known as Diagram 100A.

The first drawings of the new locomotive showed a boiler pressure of 220lb/sq in, following that of the 'A3' Pacifics, which together with 20in×26in cylinders and 6ft 2in coupled wheels, resulted in a tractive effort of 26,281lb. However, Thompson wanted his new engine to have a higher tractive effort than that of the 'Black Fives', which he was told was 26,520lb, and consequently the boiler pressure was arbitrarily raised to 225lb/sq in, giving a tractive effort of 26,878lb. In the event, his advisers were in error, as the figure quoted was that of the 'Patriot' class, not that of the 'Black Five', which at 25,455lb was well under that originally conceived for the 'B1'. It is not known whether the mistake was ever brought to notice, but that is said to be the reason for settling on a boiler pressure which was then new to the LNER, but which was to be applied to a number of subsequent classes. It also demonstrates the inconsequential reasons on which locomotive design sometimes depended. Moreover, whether Thompson realised it or not, the equivalent Great Western 'Hall' class, with a tractive effort of 27,273lb, had the edge over both the 'B1' and the 'Black Five', at least so far as this theoretical power calculation was concerned. However, the ability of a locomotive to haul a train depends on other factors, as was demonstrated when in testing at Swindon the 'B1' was found to produce more horsepower at the drawbar than a 'Hall', for a similar steaming rate.

The choice of 20in×26in for the two cylinders sprang from Gresley's adoption of these dimensions for his early 2-6-0s, and these may be contrasted with the 18½×28in of the 'Black Fives', which provided slightly less swept volume. Churchward had

Left:
The first of Thompson's 'B1s' spent most of its time at Stratford, moving to Doncaster in 1959. Originally No 8301, seen here as No 1000 and finally No 61000, *Springbok* is pausing at Manningtree on 12 July 1947 with the 8.48am train from Harwich Town to Liverpool Street.
G. R. Mortimer

Right:
The 'B1s' were the first new locomotives on Great North of Scotland metals since T. E. Heywood's last two 4-4-0s in 1921. They took over the main workings from the 'B12s', lasting until the end of steam in Scotland. No 61346, built at Gorton in 1949, is a very tight fit on the turntable at Keith on 17 May 1955. The graffiti on the side of the cylinder is critical of Kittybrewster's inability to clean 'this nag'.
John Robertson

been a protagonist of long piston strokes — as great as 30in in the 'Halls' and other classes — and no doubt he was followed in this by Stanier, although to a lesser extent. The smaller diameter permitted a similar reduction in the overall width of the locomotive at the cylinders, but at the expense of higher piston speeds. However, the Swindon design did not take advantage of this as the main reason why the 'Halls' had such limited route availability outside their parent system was their excessive width over the cylinders. The question of optimum length of piston stroke is another aspect of steam locomotive design never to be resolved satisfactorily.

Although not fitted to the first batch of 'B1s', an important refinement was the addition of a small electricity generator, charging a battery which provided a 6V supply for headlamp lighting, so that the enginemen could switch on the appropriate headcode at will, as well as enjoying the benefit of instrument lighting in the cab. To denote the headcode during daylight hours the intention was to use white discs of rather smaller size than those in use on the Great Eastern section. However, the generators proved to be a source of trouble, and there were many failures. The first examples were driven directly from the rear axle of the bogie, but these were prone to falling off, and a trial order for five steam operated sets was placed in June 1946, the price being £1,420. These were evidently satisfactory at first and most of the class were fitted with them, the mounting being on the right-hand running plate ahead of the steam pipe cover. However, many went into disuse as the engines grew older and resort had to be made to conventional oil-burning headlamps placed on abnormally long lamp irons, above the electric ones. A detail change was the substitution of a sideways-operating Robinson regulator handle, in place of the Gresley pull-out type. This was received with mixed feelings, depending upon which variety a particular driver preferred.

The tenders provided for the 'B1s' were of the standard LNER 4,200gal type, although minor design alterations took place on occasion. These were the normal accompaniment to all Gresley's tender engines except for the largest classes such as the Pacifics, and certain smaller ones for which a version carrying 3,500gal was sufficient. However, in early BR days, four coal-weighing tenders were specially built, and these moved around amongst various members of the class, as indeed did many of the standard ones. The precise reasons for the construction of these special tenders have not been explained, nor have any results been published of tests in which they were used; indeed it does not appear that they were in constant use. So far as is known, no 'B1s' ever ran with a Great Northern coal-rail tender, or with a short Great Eastern one.

Thompson received authority to construct the initial batch of 10 'B1s' in July 1942, and it is evident that a good deal of preparatory work had been done before then, as the first of the class, No 8301, left Darlington in the following December. This would have been good going in normal times, but in the pressures of wartime it was quite remarkable. However, a lesser effort went into construction of the remainder of the batch, as the last was not completed until June 1944 — 18 months after the first. Concurrently with the 'B1s', Darlington was busy with building badly-needed 'V2s' as well as a variety of war material.

No more of the class were authorised until Thompson had received Board approval for his postwar programme. In this he postulated a total of 1,000 engines of 10 classes to be built over the five-year period between 1 January 1946 and 31 December 1950, of which 400 would be 'B1s'. A similar number of old engines were to be withdrawn, eliminating 49 of the 158 classes then in existence. The proposals were qualified by the proviso that the development of diesel or diesel-electric locomotives might affect the building of steam engines, but no mention was made of possible electrification. This was the only instance in the LNER's history in which such a long-term strategy could be implemented, the company's chronic cash shortage having prevented anything on these lines from being put together in earlier years. However, finance was now available from the Arrears of Maintenance Fund accumulated by the Government

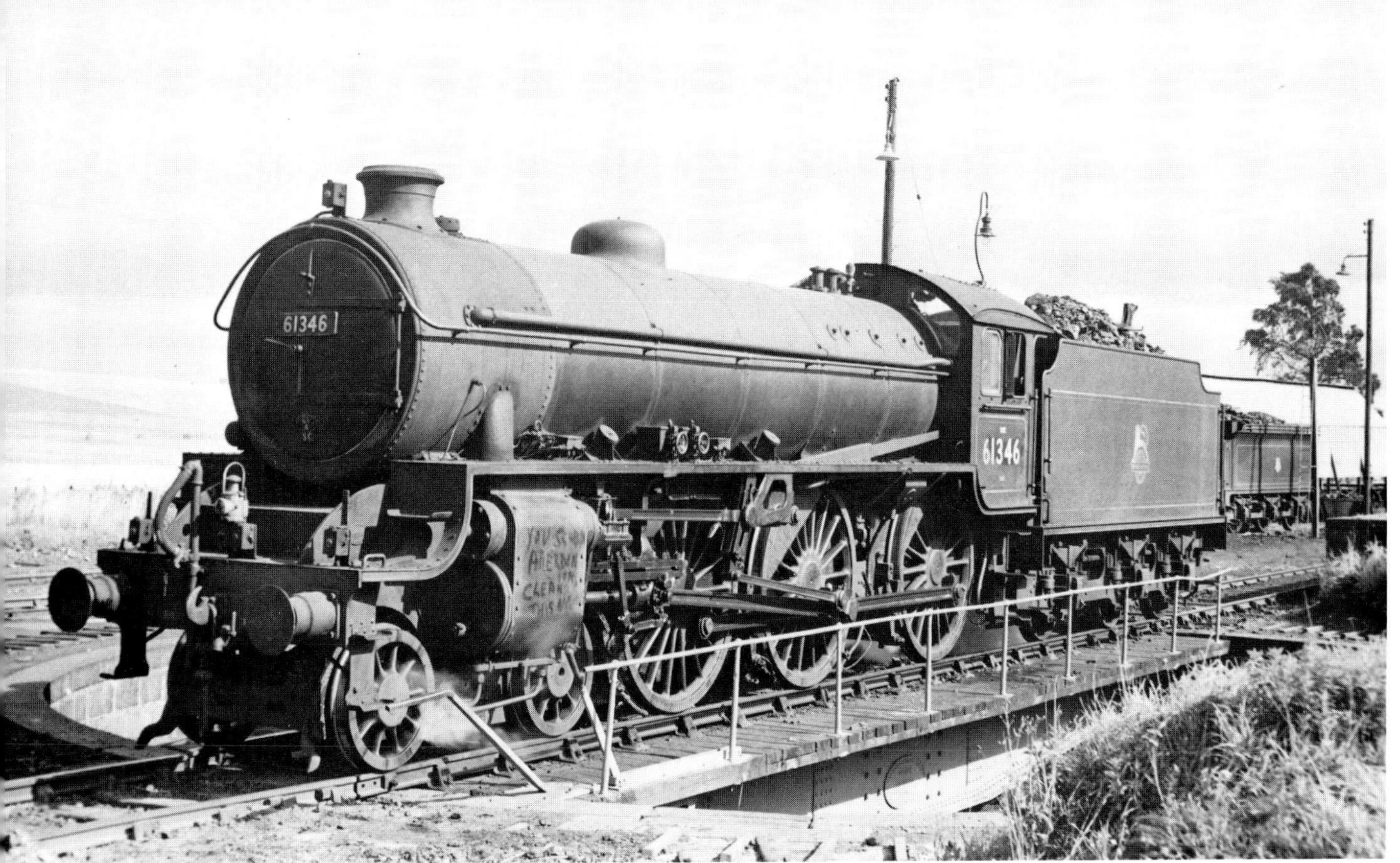

over the war years, during which the railways had received scant recognition of the invaluable work carried out whilst they were under Government control. In the event, the 400 'B1s' were all delivered, which considering the circumstances was a splendid achievement; there inevitably was some slippage before the final total was reached, the last not being received into traffic until April 1952, over four years after the LNER had succumbed to Nationalisation.

The five-year plan was pre-empted to a small extent, as 30 'B1s' for construction at Darlington were included in the 1945 locomotive building programme. However, once the Board had approved the five-year plan, substantial orders were placed with NBL, the largest locomotive builders in Britain, and the Vulcan Foundry. No fewer than 250 were ordered from NBL, in two stages, at a contract price of £14,895 each; Vulcan charged £15,300 each for 50. Once the builders got into their stride, delivery was rapid, 78 being delivered in 1946 and as many as 186 in 1947; completion was speeded by the construction of boilers at Darlington and Gorton, which produced 50 between them. Two small lots of 'B1s' were ordered in the last months of the LNER's independent existence, 10 from Darlington and 10 from Gorton, but the remainder had to await sanction from the British Transport Commission. Nevertheless, this was forthcoming, and 40 more came from NBL, inflation having forced the unit price up to £16,190, whilst a final 10 were built at Darlington. All 410 were never in service at the same time, however, as No 61057 was withdrawn after a collision in foggy conditions at Witham in March 1950.

Thompson told his Board that the 'B1s' were intended as replacements for all the older LNER 4-6-0, 2-6-0, 4-4-2 and 4-4-0 classes, as well as 0-6-0s such as the 'J39s' which took their turn on excursion work. In fact, things did not quite turn out that way, as not enough were built, and they did not nearly match in numbers even the obsolete large-wheeled passenger engines. However, to demonstrate its versatility, when it was new, the first, No 8301, was tried on a variety of workings in various parts of the country, before being allocated to Stratford. The most urgent need for the new engines was on the Great Eastern, as the 'Claud Hamilton' 4-4-0s were on their last legs and wartime traffic had placed severe stress on the locomotive fleet generally. Consequently, eight of the first 10 were allocated to sheds in East Anglia, as well as the first 20 of those built in 1946. Within a year or two the 'B1s' had taken over virtually all the best turns on the GE system, and at Nationalisation 43 of the 274 then in service were allocated to the four main sheds in that section.

Once the immediate needs of the Great Eastern were met, attention was turned to the Great Central, where all the Robinson express passenger classes of prewar days were in need of replacement. By 1949 some 90 'B1s' were posted to sheds from Neasden to Gorton and Immingham, so that for a time virtually all fast and many secondary trains were worked by the new engines. Later, as new Peppercorn 'A1s' released older Gresley Pacifics, some of these returned to the Great Central to take over the more important jobs, but these engines were not in the peak of condition when they arrived at their new sheds, and a 'B1' frequently had to deputise for a Pacific which was not in the best of health.

Other early allocations were to King's Cross and Hitchin, as replacements for Ivatt Atlantics on outer suburban and Cambridge services, and although the GN section was well provided with 'V2s', both New England and Doncaster sheds received numbers of 'B1s'. As the Pacifics and 'V2s' were too heavy for the Peterborough-Grimsby line, 'B1s' from New England and Immingham operated both passenger and freight (including fish) traffic on this part of the system. Most of the main GN sheds had an allocation, which in addition to local secondary workings often found employment on excursion trains to the coast or to London.

The widespread North Eastern Area received relatively fewer 'B1s', partly because, unlike other prewar 4-6-0s, the 'B16s' continued in service until the 1960s. A small allocation was made to the major sheds, but no more than 56 were there at

Nationalisation. When all the class were in service, in April 1952, the Region, as it was then styled, possessed 80 which were widely distributed throughout the system. Early arrivals at Neville Hill replaced 'D49' 4-4-0s on workings to Newcastle, Hull and Scarborough, whilst those at Botanic Gardens worked passenger trains to Doncaster, Leeds, Scarborough, Sheffield and York. The Gateshead allocation shared the Carlisle line workings with 'B1s' from Canal shed, those at Darlington had passenger duties to Newcastle, Leeds and York, whilst the York 'B1s' covered services to Sheffield, Leeds, Scarborough and Lincoln. Tweedmouth had a small allocation working three main line turns to Newcastle and Edinburgh, whilst during the summer months the class was used extensively on excursion and Saturday-Only trains, some reaching as far west as Blackpool, Morecambe and even Llandudno. Some North Eastern depots used their 'B1s' on freight duties. Dairycoates shed at Hull had charge of braked goods trains to York and fish trains to Doncaster but those at Borough Gardens and Stockton were used mainly on shorter-distance freight duties. York had a through turn to Liverpool, and Darlington was responsible for nine daily freights to Tyneside and York.

Two of the original 10 were sent to Scotland, being employed on Edinburgh-Perth trains. More were later allocated to the Scottish Area, notably to Kittybrewster, where they replaced worn-out 'B12s' on the Great North of Scotland services — and incidentally they were the first new locomotives to be seen north of Aberdeen since the last of the Heywood 4-4-0s in 1921. In time they came to be seen all over the North British system, including the West Highland line, taking the place of the oldest North British 4-4-0s.

By 1950, when the last of the Peppercorn 'A1' Pacifics had been delivered, the locomotive stock available for front line passenger and fast goods work on the ex-LNER system totalled 202 Pacifics, 183 'V2s' and No 60700, the erstwhile 'Hush-hush' — a total of 386 'Big Engines' in BR Power Classes 7 and 8. This impressive fleet was backed up by smaller mixed traffic engines of the 'K3' and 'B16' classes, plus, by that date, some 360 'B1s'. One would have thought that the larger engines would have been sufficient for the main workings all over the system, but this was not the case, as not only were they prohibited from most of the Great Eastern system, but certain sheds were provided with nothing more powerful than 'B1s'. Consequently, despite their limitations — and there was a considerable diffference in capability between a 'B1' and a 'V2', for example — the Thompson 4-6-0s hauled a number of important services, some

Below:
After the LMR shed at Canklow, near Rotherham, was transferred to the North Eastern Region on 1 January 1957, it acquired a small number of 'B1s', including No 61039 *Steinbok*, the last of the batch of 30 built at Darlington in 1946-47. The engine is seen here on the ash pits at Holbeck MPD on 24 January 1964. Originally provided with a tender from a North Eastern Atlantic, this had been replaced by the group standard 4,200gal version. *John K. Morton*

Left and below:
Good front end detail can be discerned in these two close-ups of 'B1s' at rest. (Left) No 61245 *Murray of Elibank* is at the ex-Caledonian shed at Dalry Road, Edinburgh on 12 June 1965. Note especially the electricity generator and cabling layout, as well as the curved fillet inserted by Cowlairs shed in the valance of the running plate. No 61245 was named after one of the Directors of the LNER. (Below) No 61306, seen at Holbeck Leeds on 23 September 1967, about to travel light to Bradford to pick up a parcels train, was withdrawn at the end of the month, fortunately to be preserved.
James A. King; John A. M. Vaughan

Left:
In May 1947, Nos 1158 and 1159, brand-new from the Vulcan Foundry, pass through Manchester London Road on their way to Gorton, where they were to be based. They carry full LNER lined green livery with unshaded sans serif characters, and electric headlamps.
C. H. S. Owen/GCR Society Collection

of them over long distances. Among them were those on the King's Cross-Grimsby route, which were handled by 'B1s' stationed at Immingham, with through workings in each direction — one being the well patronised 4.00pm from King's Cross. These frequently loaded to 12 bogies, and timekeeping was not always of the highest order; operating delays were the main reason and, despite the easy road and generous schedules, the 'B1s' were not always able to recover time lost in checks. Nevertheless this arrangement continued for about 12 years, until the allocation of new Type 4 diesels to Stratford permitted surplus 'Britannia' Pacifics to be used on these important trains.

Another difficult task, but more within the capability of the 'B1s', was the postwar 'East Anglian', which was in the hands of members of the class stationed at Norwich. This train was reinstated in the winter timetable of 1946-47, with its prewar six-coach formation strengthened by an additional two bogies and the schedule extended by 10min. Two years later the 'Norfolkman', a corresponding service running down in the morning and returning in the early evening, was introduced and entrusted to haulage by Stratford 'B1s'.

The initial batch of 'B1s' were numbered from 8301 to 8310. To maintain continuity in numbering, as it was foreseen even then that the class would be extensively replicated, it was proposed to renumber ex-GER locomotives occupying numbers in the 83xx, 84xx and 85xx series into other blank areas in the GER block. The main engines affected were the 'B12s', and those were allocated the numbers 7415 to 7494. However, the comprehensive scheme devised in 1943 and implemented in 1946 overtook this proposal, and only a dozen or so actually received their interim numbers. The original 10 'B1s' received their 1946 numbers early in that year, becoming Nos 1000 to 1009, and subsequent construction brought the series up to 1409, although well before the last engine appeared (it was actually No 61399) the BR addition of 60,000 was being applied. Nevertheless, despite the proclaimed intention to build a further 400 of the class as part of the postwar building programme, insufficient allowance was made for these in the 1946 renumbering, and GCR and NER 4-6-0s originally given numbers in the 1300s and 1400s had to be renumbered once more, higher in the sequence, to make way for later 'B1s'.

The pioneer of the class, No 8301 was named *Springbok*, reportedly in honour of General Smuts, then Premier of the Union of South Africa, and all except one of the first 41 were given names of varieties of wild deer. The rationale behind the choice is not easy to discover, as the class were not to be noted for their speed or agility, and most of the names (see Appendix 1) were incomprehensible to the staff and public alike. One unfortunate engine, No 1005, bore the name *Bongo* and gave its name unofficially to the class generally, although an attempt was made by the management to have them known as the 'Antelope' class. One of the 1946-47 Darlington batch, and 17 of those built in 1947, were given names of members of the LNER Board. (The Chairmen, Deputy Chairmen and Chairman of the Locomotive Committee had already been commemorated in the 'A4' class.) Again, these names possessed little public relations value, although for their first postings the engines concerned were stationed in the area in which the particular director resided. For some reason, the name of the Hon Rupert Beckett was not amongst those recalled in this way, although he was one of only five directors to have served the LNER throughout its existence. Of the others, Alexander Reith Gray and Oliver Bury died before they were able to see the locomotives named after them. (Bury had had an illustrious railway career, having been General Manager of the Great Northern Railway before being elected to the Board of the GNR and later that of the LNER.) One of the last 'B1s' to be built, No 61379, was given the name *Mayflower* to commemorate the close ties between Boston in Lincolnshire and Boston, Massachusetts — this having been the name of the sailing ship which had carried a party of settlers to New England 300 years before. No 61379 was shedded at Immingham and worked regular, as well as a number of special trains, between King's Cross and Boston, although from all accounts it was not one of the best of the class. As representative of a late generation of steam locomotives, the 'B1s' found their work steadily eroded by the rising tide of electric and diesel motive power. The first inroads followed the completion of the Manchester, Sheffield and Wath electrification in 1954 which resulted in electric traction replacing steam haulage on Trans-Pennine passenger trains travelling via this route, many of which were formerly worked by 'B1s'. The introduction of diesel mechanical multiple-unit trains on cross-country, branch and main line stopping trains in the later 1950s led to the loss of many steam-hauled services, as did the introduction of the several new diesel locomotive types under the modernisation plan. However, these early units were not as reliable as had been expected, and steam in the shape of a 'B1' often provided a hasty substitute.

Another factor affecting the careers of the 'B1s' was the introduction in 1951 of 'Britannia' Pacifics on the Liverpool Street services, whilst inter-Regional transfers brought engines from other regions into what had previously been LNER territory. Conversely 'B1s' were often to be seen on the lines of

the other 'Big Four' companies. This was notably the case in Scotland, where establishment of one Region to cover both the LNER and LMS systems north of the border led to a certain amount of cross-posting. For instance 'Black Fives' were seen on the West Highland line, and 'B1s' appeared on the Glasgow & South Western. Other transfers included allocations to Carstairs and Dalry Road, Edinburgh, working from the latter over the Caledonian route to Glasgow, filling in on the Cathcart circle, where it was not unknown for them to operate tender first. After the transfer of the Great Central London Extension to the London Midland Region, 'Royal Scots' and 'Black Fives' replaced 'B1s' and other LNER classes on many services. A most interesting inter-Regional loan took place in May 1953 when 14 of the class were sent to Stewart's Lane to work on the Kent coast services during a period when the Bulleid Pacifics had been temporarily taken out of service for axle examination.

In the well publicised locomotive exchanges held in the summer of 1948, the LNER was represented in the express passenger engine category by Gresley's 'A4' Pacifics. This left the 'B1s' taking part in the mixed traffic class as the only LNER representatives of the 4-6-0 type. The locomotives chosen were Nos 61163, 61251 *Oliver Bury*, a King's Cross engine well known to local commuters, and 61292. They were seen on passenger trains on the Great Western between Bristol and Plymouth, on the LMS between St Pancras and Manchester and between Perth and Inverness, and on the Great Central line from Marylebone to Manchester.

The trials generated widespread interest, probably more so among enthusiasts than among railwaymen themselves. However, variations in such important factors as driving practice, the weather, operating conditions and quality of coal were too great to average out, so that although the trials were documented in detail, and informed comment was later published by Cecil J. Allen, no clear evidence was produced which proved conclusively that any one of the three mixed traffic 4-6-0 classes was 'better' than its rivals. The objective of the trials was said to be the identification of the best features of each class, so that these could be incorporated in the proposed BR Standard designs, which were then under consideration. In the event, little emerged to convince the BR design team that their reliance on the main LMS features was misplaced, but this is not to say that had Doncaster been in the driving seat instead of Derby, a Standard '5' based on the 'B1' would not have been the equal of the locomotive that eventually appeared. Nevertheless, two important LNER details from the 'B1' were incorporated in the Standard design. These were the later Gresley type of three-bar

Top:
One of the earliest LNER locomotives to be identified with British Railways, No E1051 is seen at Stratford on 7 February 1948. The livery appears to be unlined black, with small handpainted letters on the tender. Note the larger-than-usual balance weights. *H. C. Casserley*

Right:
Existing on borrowed time after withdrawal, No 61252 was employed as a stationary boiler for carriage heating purposes at Ipswich on 16 February 1964. Renumbered 22 in service stock, the significance of the '91' is unknown. Most of these conversions had their drawgear removed, but this one has only lost its coupling. *H. N. James*

slide bar, instead of the heavier two-bar type favoured by Stanier, and the adoption of the LNER coupled wheel dimension of 6ft 2in. Doncaster was in fact the parent office for the design of the Standard '5s', but had little influence in the matter — the principles and main dimensions having been laid down by Riddles and Cox.

In what would have been one of the few detailed investigations carried out at the newly commissioned Locomotive Testing Station at Rugby, 'B1' No 61353 was to have been tried with alternative blast pipe and chimney arrangements, but in the event no modifications were carried out. However, together with a series of road trials on the Settle to Carlisle line, during which, for unexplained reasons, the locomotive was not indicated, some testing was put in hand at Rugby in 1950-52, the results of which broadly indicated that with correct firing the exhaust arrangements as designed could not be improved. Moreover, the tests showed that, when fired with average quality Blidworth coal at a constant rate of 3,000lb/hr, the output of the 'B1' exceeded those of the 'Black Five' and the 'Hall'. Thus, presumably because of the satisfactory trials with No 61353, none of the class was ever fitted with a basically different blast system such as a Kylchap, or with a double chimney; nor was one put through the test plant at Swindon, where investigations by the renowned Sammy Ell had resulted in marked improvements in the steaming of other classes. Incidentally, one of G. J. Churchward's criteria for an express passenger locomotive was that it should be capable of exerting a drawbar pull of 2 tons at 70mph. The 'B1' was recorded as having achieved this standard whilst being fired with Blidworth coal at a rate of 2,450lb/hr. Apart from the premature withdrawal of No 61057 in 1951, the first 'B1' to go was No 61085 in November 1961, and from then on withdrawals came steadily. The last one went in 1967, although a few of the class had their lives extended by a couple of years through being used as mobile carriage heating boilers. The last areas of steam in Britain were in the west and northwest, and it was from these localities that the majority of locomotives found their way to Woodham's Yard at Barry, particularly after that decisive weekend in 1968 when diesels took over the last workings from steam. Dieselisation had been completed earlier on the LNER system, and consequently virtually all the 'B1s' had been withdrawn well before the final holocaust and were scrapped — mainly by contractors — soon after withdrawal. Of these, 120 went in 1952, 62 in 1963, 53 in 1964, 82 in 1965, 64 in 1966, and the last 27 went in 1967. Fortunately, two have been preserved. Gerald Boden is the owner of No 1306, fully restored to running order on the Great Central Railway at Loughborough; it is resplendent in lined LNER green and has been given the name *Mayflower*. No 1264, also at Loughborough, is being restored by the Thompson 'B1' Locomotive Trust.

Although overwhelmingly the most important, the 'B1s' were not Edward Thompson's only essay into the 4-6-0 type. After his accession, in addition to looking forward to his own individual contribution to locomotive design, he reviewed a number of older LNER classes to see how these could be fitted into his plans for the future. In particular he seems to have had in mind the rebuilding of older engines into the virtual equivalent of his 'B1', but with larger diameter wheels. The opportunity to carry this out in practice first occurred in 1943, when No 6166, one of the Caprotti-fitted Robinson 'B3s' cracked a cylinder, and as other heavy repairs were needed, Thompson evidently thought that the cost of major reconstruction was worthwhile. What was actually involved in money terms has not been disclosed, nor — unlike his more controversial rebuilding of the 'P2s' — did the project come before the Locomotive Committee. With its modern valve and front end design, the rebuild should have been a big improvement, but No 6166 was reportedly unsuccessful in its new form, and lasted less than six years before being withdrawn, giving a poor return on the money spent on its reconstruction. Initially based at Gorton, it was later moved to Neasden and worked on Marylebone trains until it was transferred to Immingham for the last two years of its existence. Little has been recorded of its work after rebuilding, but one report describes an occasion on which it stalled in the Woodhead tunnel. The driver, confused by the unfamiliar controls, set back when he thought he was in forward gear, and ran into the train following. No other 'B3s' were rebuilt in the same way, and No 6166 remained the sole representative of its class, receiving the sub-classification of 'B3/3'.

Thompson's next essay into the 4-6-0 field took place two years later, although, almost since the date of his appointment, he had given consideration to rebuilding certain of Gresley's three-cylinder locomotives into two-cylinder form, with his

Below:
Four tenders with facilities for weighing coal were specially built in 1951-52 and used with a number of members of the 'B1' class. No 61140 is seen at Eastfield shed, Glasgow, on 19 April 1954 with one of these tenders, which three months later was transferred to No 61172. It is not known what information about coal consumption was obtained from their use. *W. A. C. Smith*

Above:
A main area of work for 'B1s' on the Great Northern section was in replacement of Ivatt Atlantics on outer suburban and Cambridge trains. They had been on these duties for 12 years when No 61314 was photographed on one such working, leaving Platform 8 at King's Cross in 1959. *M. S. Welch*

standard 20in × 26in outside cylinders. The first of these was the 'K3' 2-6-0 No 206, which was converted at Doncaster in June 1945, with a 6ft diameter boiler similar to that fitted originally, but with the pressure raised to 225lb/sq in. This was followed two months later by one of the 'B17s' — again selected because it was in need of major repairs. The resulting locomotive was very similar to No 6166 (the only visible difference of any consequence was in the wheel spacing) and was virtually a 6ft 8in version of the 'B1', although in this case it was reclassified 'B2' and not merely given a sub-classification. In appearance, the outlines of both the 'B3/3' and the 'B2' were sharpened, the reverse curves characteristic of Doncaster practice being replaced by a higher running plate with the typical Darlington quadrants, as on the 'B1s'. The coupled wheels were not completely exposed, however, as miniscule splashers were provided as on the 'B3/3'. A very slight difference may be detected in the size of the splashers, possibly attributable to the nominal 1in difference in the wheel diameters.

The first 'B17' to be converted, in what was in effect a renewal of almost every component except the frames and wheels, was No 2871 *Manchester City*, which was the last but one to have entered service, this having occurred only eight years before. Ten conversions were authorised and these went through the works as opportunity offered, the last emerging in 1949. No further 'B17s' were subjected to such drastic treatment however, as a less costly modification resulted from a straightforward replacement of the original boiler by one of the later '100As'. This, incidentally, had the merit of increasing the locomotive's tractive effort by some 12%. Apart from those rebuilt as 'B2s', all except six of the 'B17s' eventually received this treatment, although on some the boiler pressure was reduced to 180lb/sq in, to ease maintenance.

Of the 'B2' conversions, only the first attracted any notice which was out of the ordinary. It was decided that this would be an appropriate locomotive for Royal train workings and consequently, a 'Footballer' being considered inappropriate, No 2871 was renamed *Royal Sovereign*. It continued on its special duties until withdrawn in 1958 and was maintained in excellent external condition. It was a familiar sight on the routes from Cambridge to King's Cross and Liverpool Street, as when not needed for Royal trains it was occupied on buffet car and other services. Otherwise, the 'B2s' did not appear to have any superiority over the original 'B17s'. Indeed, the rebuilds, which were equipped with 100A boilers and retained the original cylinder arrangements, were said to have been better — this being confirmed by dynamometer car trials on the Colchester main line in 1947. The greater stresses induced by the operation of two cylinders instead of three, in an already weak frame, led to repetitive cracking faults — No 1671 suffering no fewer than seven. All the 'B2s' were withdrawn by the end of 1959.

However, this was not quite the full story of Edward Thompson's 4-6-0s, as in addition to the 'B16' conversions described in Chapter 2, he had ideas for rebuilding the Great Central 'B7s' with the Diagram 100A boiler and 20in × 26in outside cylinders — virtually as a 5ft 8in version of the 'B1'. Whether this would have been any more successful than the original Robinson design is open to conjecture, in view of the record of No 6166, as in the event, although the matter was gone into in some depth, nothing was to come of it.

Finally, 10 years after Thompson's retirement, a serious proposal was made to replace the '100A' boiler of the 'B1s' by the BR3 type, as fitted to the BR Standard '5' 4-6-0s. This, with its Belpaire firebox and tapered boiler, would have radically altered these features of the original — not because of any engineering problem, but because of alleged maintenance difficulties with the '100A' firebox. Again, nothing came of the proposal.

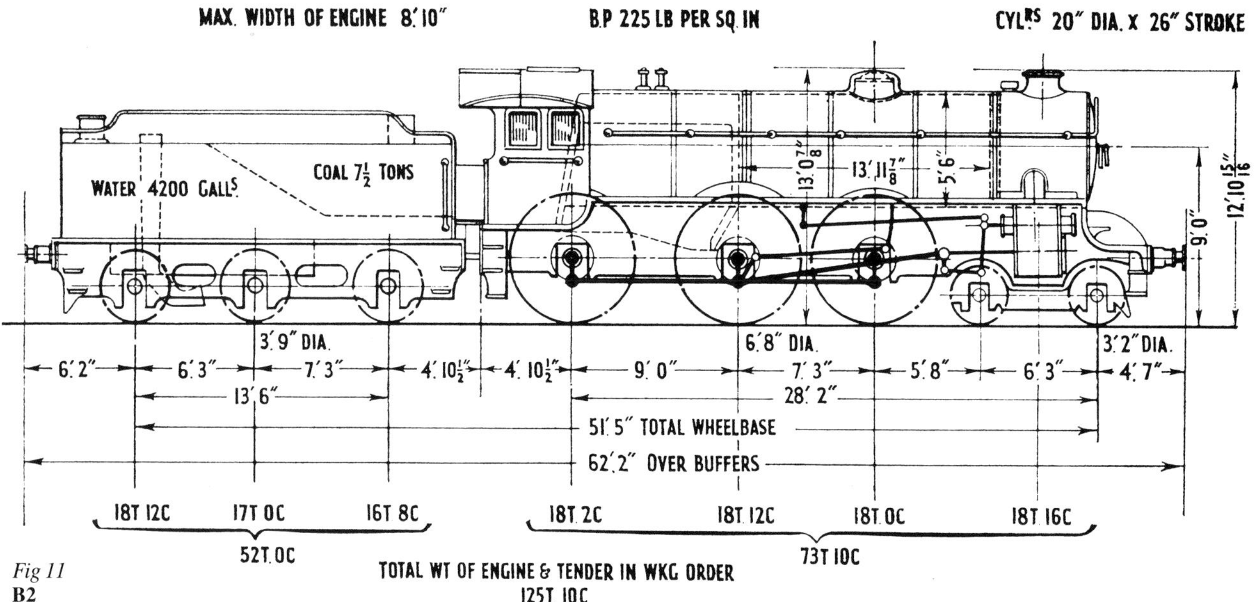

Fig 11
B2

Below:
No 1003 *Gazelle* was one of the first locomotives to receive the new unshaded sans serif numbers and letters, and is seen leaving Platform 9 at Liverpool Street station with the 8.00pm 'Hook Continental' on 29 July 1947. Running Foreman Arthur Davey is at the platform end.
C. C. B. Herbert

Right:
The last scheduled steam arrival into Liverpool Street was an evening boat train from Parkeston Quay on Sunday 9 September 1962, headed by 'B1' No 61156. The Great Eastern section was one of the first areas of British Railways to dispense with steam, all services being hauled by electric or diesel traction by the end of 1963. *BR*

Below right:
Although not delivered by NBL until after Nationalisation, 'B1' No 1282 is still in LNER livery on 5 June 1948. The engine appears nicely cleaned, although, judging by the scorching, with an ill-fitting smokebox door. It is seen heading a special train for Nottingham, passing Colwick.
T. Newbould

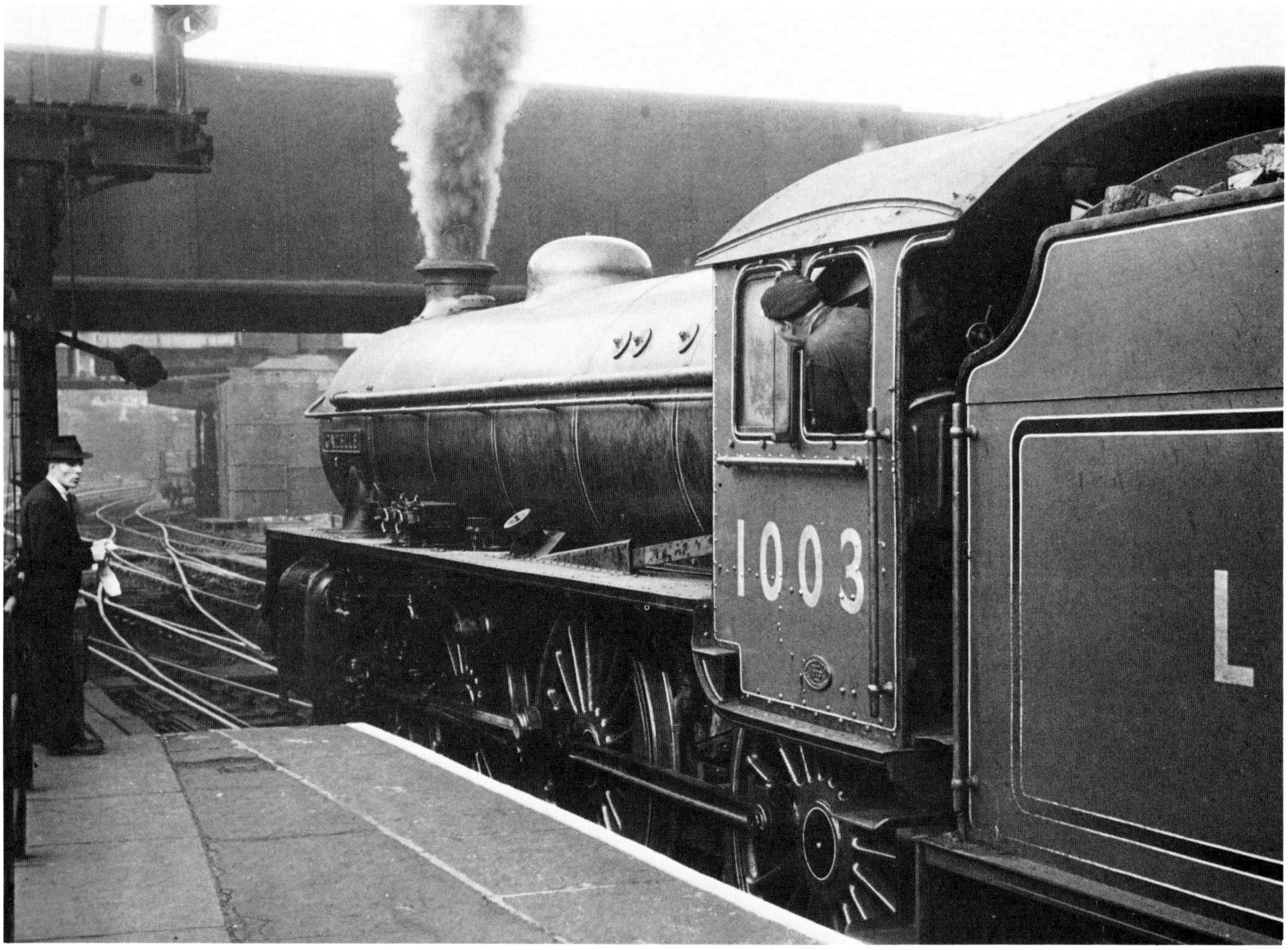

61156
61156
30A
SUNDAY TELEGRAPH
FEATURES THE BEST IN SUNDAY READING

306
L N E R
1282
No 1282

This picture:
To see a double-headed express on the Great Northern main line was usually a sign of trouble, as in this instance on 7 July 1951. 'A3' No 60108 *Gay Crusader* failed at Knebworth with the 8.25am (SO) from Newcastle, and 'B1' No 61113 of King's Cross shed was called on to give assistance. The train is emerging from the southern end of Hadley South tunnel, passing the splitting signals controlling the recommencement of four tracks, before the Potters Bar widening had taken place.
E. D. Bruton

Below:
The Saturdays-Only 'Butlin's Express' is seen entering Sandy station, on the Great Northern main line, in August 1960, headed by 'B1' No 61302. This was a summer season Second Class only train carrying holidaymakers from King's Cross to Skegness, and returning with others whose holiday had ended. *John C. Baker*

This picture:
A nice study of railwaymen and passengers at Leicester London Road station on 9 July 1957. The 'B1s' took over many cross-country services previously worked by old engines which were due for scrapping, and continued on this work until DMUs took over or the services were withdrawn. Here, No 61323 has just arrived with the 9.16am train from Peterborough East via Melton Mowbray and Syston. The engine had only recently been transferred from the Scottish Region; note the fillets in the angle of the running plate. *D. C. Ovenden*

Below:
The south end of York station in 1949, with No 61337 of Neville Hill shed in charge of a train bound for Leeds. In the left background are two oil storage tanks installed for an abortive oil firing scheme.
Ian Allan Library

61370

Left:
One of the last batch of 'B1s' built by NBL No 61370 is hauling the 3.30pm stopping train from Manchester Central to Sheffield between Marple and Strines on the Great Central & Midland Joint line on 22 May 1964. *A. Moyes*

Above:
Nicely photographed on the Forth Bridge in August 1949, No 61178 appears in LNER green. It bears the full title of its new owners on the tender, a smokebox numberplate, but no shedplate. *Wethersett Collection/Ian Allan Library*

Right:
No 61084 of York shed is seen entering Newcastle Central over the famed crossing at the east end of the station, in 1948. The train is from Liverpool, and is composed of Stanier stock in early British Railways livery. *Real Photos*

61177

Far left:
A regular Pullman working for the 'B1,' was the 'Queen of Scots' between Glasgow Queen Street and Edinburgh Waverley. In July 1959, No 61243 *Sir Harold Mitchell* is approaching Waverley through the picturesque surroundings of Princes Street Gardens. Sir Harold himself was a Director of the LNER representing Scottish interests. Amongst many other activities he was a Member of Parliament, took a close interest in Anglo-Polish relations, and was a skier of international class.
L. Perrin/Gresley Society Collection

Far left, bottom:
'B1s' were employed to the full on excursion jobs, such as this working from Kirkby-in-Ashfield to Mablethorpe. No 61177 is pulling out of Mansfield on 2 August 1958 — the Sunday before the Bank Holiday, in the days when it occurred at the beginning of August. Note the Thompson coaches, distinguished by the oval toilet windows.
J. Cupit

Top left:
No 61189 *Sir William Gray*, having lost its nameplates, is in charge of the Bradford portion of a train from King's Cross to Leeds and Bradford in October 1964. The coaches were detached at Wakefield and followed the remainder of the train as far as Copley Hill, where the train turned west on to the line from Leeds to Bradford Exchange. Ardsley shed is in the distance.
S. W. Banks

Above left:
A down train in the Menassie Gorge, east of Roy Bridge on the West Highland line, in the summer of 1948. No 61326 is in charge of seven bogies, not far now from its destination Fort William. *Ian Allan Library*

Left:
In the summer season, 'B1s' regularly worked from Glasgow Queen Street to Oban, via Crianlarich. Here No 61344 of Eastfield shed is approaching Connel Ferry on 7 July 1949, the fireman ready to hand over the single line token. *G. W. Goslin*

Above:
As the 'B1s' were completed by NBL, they were delivered to Eastfield, who often used them for a short time to supplement their own allocation. In August 1947, brand-new No 1222, is seen on an officers special climbing the 1 in 67 towards Corrour station on the West Highland, a section of line inaccessible by public transport. The engine was shortly to be allocated to Carlisle Canal shed, where it remained until withdrawal in 1962. *Ian Allan Library*

Three photographs of 'B1s' in company with mixed traffic locomotives of other railways:

Below:
No 61394 is seen entering Wembley Hill on 30 March 1957 with a return excursion to Newark and Doncaster, whilst on the opposite platform is GWR No 4949 *Packwood Hall* about to leave for Taunton. The occasion was a Schoolboys International soccer match at Wembley Stadium. Note the GWR, LNER and GCR signals. *C. R. L. Coles*

Above:
Prior to the introduction of the 'Britannias', trials of a Southern Railway 'Battle of Britain' Pacific took place between Liverpool Street and Norwich. No 34059 *Sir Archibald Sinclair* which was waiting to work the up 'Norfolkman' on 18 May 1949 is seen standing alongside 'B1' No 61058, in Norwich loco yard. *C. C. B. Herbert*

Below:
An LMS 'Black Five' and an LNER 'B1' stand side by side at Scarborough on 3 September 1966. No 44896 had arrived on the last regular steam working from Wakefield, the 9.12am, and was to work back home light engine. 'B1' No 61030 *Nyala* was waiting to return to Halifax with a works outing special. *O. D. Taylor*

Left:
No 61251 *Oliver Bury* took part in the 1948 locomotive trials as one of the representatives of LNER practice in the mixed traffic category. Here it is seen leaving Plymouth North Road on 7 July 1948, accompanied by the GWR dynamometer car. Oliver Bury was well known as a General Manager of the Great Northern Railway, later becoming a Director not only of that company but later of the LNER.
Stephenson Locomotive Society Collection

Above:
When new in July 1946, LNER No 1055 was allocated to Ipswich and remained there when Richard Hardy, the author of the Foreword, was shedmaster. As British Railways No 61055, it is seen at 3.30am on 4 January 1964, while acting as station pilot at Sheffield Victoria. *J. C. Haydon*

Left:
As the 'B17s' (and Ivatt Atlantics) had done in earlier years, 'B1s' regularly ventured on to the Great Western system. Here, in rather sooty postwar green, and in company with Gresley stock, No 1123 is seen at Oxford with the 9.20am from Sheffield to Swansea on 9 March 1947. During this period the engine worked through from Leicester to Swindon.
R. H. G. Simpson

Left:
On 20 July 1948, the 8.25am from Manchester to Marylebone grossed some 350 tons, and was double-headed in its final stages by a pair of 'B1s'. The train is seen approaching Marylebone in the care of Nos 61163 and 61111, in LNER lined green but renumbered.
LCGB/Ken Nunn Collection

Left and below:
'B1s' were often to be seen on named expresses, but not normally the 'Tees-Tyne Pullman'; No 61207 of New England shed is deputising for a failed Pacific on 12 August 1953 (left). However, the class generally worked 'The Master Cutler' in its inaugural year, and No 1223 (below) is hauling the train, the 7.15am Sheffield-Marylebone, over Metropolitan electrified track near North Harrow on 13 October 1947.
Allan Garraway; LCGB/ Ken Nunn Collection

Above:
A rather grimy No 61207 is seen in distinguished company, hauling Ivatt Atlantic No 251 and Stirling Single No 1 through Grantham station en route to the Railway Museum at York on 21 October 1952.
LCGB/Ken Nunn Collection

Below:
The 'B1s' were not often seen on through goods workings in the King's Cross area, and this illustration of No 1112 hauling a down fitted freight in the summer of 1947 is exceptional. The engine, seen on the two-track bottleneck through Hadley Wood, was probably deputising for a 'V2'.
M. W. Earley

Right:
No 61017 *Bushbuck* bustles along with a down fitted freight near Charwelton on the Great Central on 18 July 1964. This is probably a Woodford to York working; the engine was stationed at Ardsley at the time. *Gerald T. Robinson*

Below right:
Eastfield's 'B1s' were as likely to be seen on the West Highland line as on the road to Edinburgh. However, the beauty of the countryside around the Perthshire/Argyll border is hidden by a Scotch mist as No 61243 *Sir Harold Mitchell* reaches the end of its climb with a freight for Fort William on 7 May 1956. *J. B. Welldon*

Above:
'B1s' occasionally penetrated the Southern Region, as on this occasion when Nos 61372 and 61317 returned from Southampton Docks with the empty stock of a boat train from Stratford. The train is passing Raynes Park on 13 October 1959, after suffering a slack due to the renewal of New Malden bridge. *G. F. Bloxam/Eric Neve Collection*

Below:
On 6 March 1965, at the site of Burton Salmon station, No 61276 starts away with a mixed goods train, after picking up three coal wagons from the adjoining sidings. The signal indicates that the train will be taking the line to Normanton. Most of the 'B1s' had been withdrawn by this time, and No 61276 had only three more months in service. *J. S. Hancock*

Right:
A trainload of precast concrete beams were on their way from St Ives to Watford, for the reconstruction of the St Albans Road bridge over the West Coast main line. The unfortunately named No 61005 *Bongo* was in charge, on 30 November 1961. The 'B1' would have worked to Cambridge, at which point an LMR engine would have taken over to complete the journey to Watford via Bletchley and Bedford St Johns. *BR*

Below right:
The engine needs cleaning but the headlamps are fresh from the paintshop as No 61127 approaches Kiveton Park with a freight for the Sheffield area on the misty morning of 18 January 1964. *Paul Riley*

Above:
'B1' No 61302 makes a vigorous climb away from the main line on to the short branch to Denton at Belvoir Junction in April 1965. In earlier years the usual engine for these iron ore workings was a Great Northern 0-6-0. *A. J. Clarke*

Below:
Empty iron ore hoppers from Stanton pass West Hallam signalbox, hauled by 'B1' No 61042, on 8 July 1964. This engine was the third of the class to be built by NBL and was one of the longest-lived, achieving almost 20 years' service. *T. Bousted*

Left:
Beautifully restored and named *Mayflower*, No 1306 powers a 'Santa Special' on the Great Central Railway near Loughborough on 15 December 1979. *R. Payne*

Above and left:
There was little of outward significance to distinguish Edward Thompson's two 4-6-0 rebuilds, which were in effect larger-wheeled versions of his 'B1'. Apart from small variations in wheel spacing, and very slight differences in the size of their miniscule splashers — indicating a minor variation in running plate height — these two locomotives have different types of tender, neither of which is the LNER group standard. 'B3/3' No 6166 (the erstwhile *Earl Haig*) (above) is seen at Gorton on completion of rebuilding in October 1943, retaining its Robinson tender, whilst 'B2' No 1616 *Fallodon*, seen at Stratford in June 1947, has the tender of withdrawn Raven 'C7' Atlantic No 733 (left).
Crown Copyright/National Railway Museum Collection (DON 43/112); E. V. Fry

Above and below:
The 'B2' which most caught the public eye was No 1671 *Royal Sovereign* which was kept in first class order specially to work the Royal trains in each direction between King's Cross and King's Lynn, en route to Wolferton station, for Sandringham. The Royal train is seen approaching Brookmans Park (above) on its way to King's Cross in the early evening of 3 June 1947 and later No 1671 is seen in the King's Cross loco yard (below). The one-time four-headlamp code denoting Royal trains was not continued after the war.
(Both) LCGB/Ken Nunn Collection

Above right:
Whilst the 'B1s' were painted black in BR days, the larger wheels of the 'B2s' qualified them for green passenger livery, although they were often used on quite minor workings. No 61616 *Fallodon* is seen leaving Cambridge on 16 June 1958 with the midday train to Colchester via Haverhill. Falloden was the country seat in Northumberland of Earl Grey, who was Foreign Secretary at the outbreak of World War 1 in 1914. He was for several years a Director of the LNER. *Frank Church*

Below right:
Still in LNER lined green on 19 February 1949, 'B2' No 61603 *Framlingham* leaves Bentley on a down parcels train. Note the NER tender, originally attached to Atlantic No 737. *G. R. Mortimer*

GOODS ENQUIRIES

BRITISH RAILWAYS
61603

7

LNER 4-6-0s: An Appreciation

The 16 disparate classes of LNER 4-6-0 form a fascinating cross-section of British examples of the type. Although each class was built to meet a particular requirement, a few, designed by different CMEs, were of similar characteristics, and some interesting comparisons can be made.

Looking first at the various 4-6-0s of the North Eastern and the Great Central, it may be noted that the two earliest NER classes had nearly all been scrapped by the early 1930s, in some cases after a life of no more than 20 years. Also, a start had been made in withdrawing the Raven 'B15s', and undoubtedly all of these would have gone within a short period had it not been for the war. Yet the three-cylinder 'B16s', both original and rebuilt, lasted almost until the end of steam. In contrast, of the 100 4-6-0s of Robinson design, all but three survived the war and a few even managed to achieve a service life of 45 years, but all, including the 'B7s' which were contemporaneous with the 'B16s' and of similar power, were gone by 1950.

One factor may have been that, despite the disparity in general dimensions of the several GCR designs, only four diagrams of boiler sufficed for the nine classes, as well as being applied to other locomotives, such as the 'O4' and 'Q4' freight engines. Another may be the robust character of Robinson's engines generally, none of which suffered premature withdrawal. Perhaps the Southern Area management was less ready to withdraw older engines than that in the North-East, although it is likely that, in face of the relentless drive to save costs, the all-line influence of the Chief Mechanical Engineer would have overcome any ideas of 'scrap and replace' whilst a locomotive class had useful life remaining.

Possibly the Great Central system offered more suitable work for which these medium power 4-6-0s were suited, rather than existed in the North-Eastern Area for their mixed traffic engines, but this does not explain the retention in service of the Raven 'B16s' for more than 10 years after the 38 Robinson 'B7s' had all gone. True, 24 of the former had been rebuilt by Gresley or Thompson, indicating that a reasonable future remained for the class, but this can only be one reason for their extended careers. The LNER standard 'K3' 2-6-0 at its best was superior to the 'B7' and 'B16' in power output and capacity for hard work — Gp Capt J. N. C. Law has estimated that the former was capable of exerting over 1,500ihp, compared with 1,250 for the 4-6-0s. However, from all accounts there was little to choose between the three classes in everyday service, but the 4-6-0s were better to ride on and did not suffer the perversities attributed to the '2 to 1' drive to the valves of the centre cylinder of a run-down 'K3'. Nevertheless, as a Group Standard class of which no fewer than 193 had been built, the 'K3s' were less likely to be withdrawn, even in early BR days, than the 38 'B7s', which by Nationalisation had generally been relegated to goods workings within the capability of the larger 0-6-0s. Another factor in the retention of the 'B16s' may have been the postwar revival of excursion working, which brought a good deal of traffic to the North-Eastern coast resorts, although it is true that much was also generated internally on the Great Central. The 'B16s' of course were ideal for this work. Interestingly, in postwar days they were often observed on workings which took them into Great Central territory, on trains on which one would have expected to have seen a 'B7'.

So far as is known, no comparative trials were ever initiated between the 'K3', 'B7' and 'B16' classes. Each represented a different school of locomotive design, and figures of performance and efficiency would have been of great interest. Whatever the outcome, Sir Nigel Gresley was too far committed to his design principles to have made any major amendments to them, but his enquiring mind would have taken note of any lesser features which such trials might have shown to have been beneficial if applied on a wider scale.

The Holden 'B12s' were never in the position of being compared with the 4-6-0s of the other LNER constituents, having been built to a specification limited in physical dimensions. They probably became the most widely travelled of all British 4-6-0s, being seen in more parts of the country even than the later BR Standard '5s'. They performed admirably on the work for which they were designed and, by taking over virtually all the more important services in the Northern Scottish Area, worked out their time on a part of the LNER system where no other class of equivalent power was permitted. Had 'B12s' not been surplus to Great Eastern section requirements in the 1930s, a completely new class would have had to be introduced for the workings north of Aberdeen. Moreover, their rebuilding as 'B12/3s' made them the virtual equivalents of the 'B17s', transforming their capability, although their nominal tractive effort remained unaltered. The 'Sandringhams' somehow rarely reached the heights expected of them, but probably any comparison with a Gresley wide-firebox class is invidious, and within their design limitations they generally performed adequately. The refusal of the North Eastern Area management to accept 'B17s' in the 1930s is probably due merely to a lack of suitable work for a medium powered but large-wheeled six-coupled engine. The subsidiary main lines, and the branch lines, in the northeast had been well engineered, and the relatively restricted route availability of the 'D49s' (RA8 in the LNER scale compared with the RA5 of the 'B17s') did not preclude them from being used on many lesser passenger workings. They were even used on the Whitby to Pickering line, although of course not over the Pennines to Kirkby Stephen. Later in the 1930s, when the North-Eastern Area could have used a larger 4-6-0 for main line work, the 'V2' met their needs.

It was a strange shortcoming on the part of the LNER management that the East Anglian services were never given locomotives with the reserve of power needed, despite the importance attached to the Parkeston Quay boat trains, and later to the Norwich services. It is therefore of interest at this stage to contemplate a Great Eastern future in which the Gresley, rather than the Thompson, influence prevailed. By the end of the 1930s, restrictions on the main lines had been relaxed to the extent that the original 180lb Pacifics, with a maximum axle weight of 20 tons, would have been permitted, subject to the easing of certain curves and the provision of 70ft turntables in selected locations. In fact no such postings took place, as during the war there was a greater need for these engines elsewhere; furthermore, as the original boilers fell due for renewal, they were replaced by the heavier 220lb boiler, so raising the axle weight to 22 tons, and hence above the limit permitted. As it was, the 'Sandringhams' and 'B12/3s' handled the main East Anglian services until the coming of the 'B1s' in quantity from 1945. However, the new locomotives did not represent any advance in power, but they had the advantage of being newly built, as distinct from engines which at best were in good condition when fresh from overhaul, but which soon deteriorated afterwards. Possibly Gresley had in mind using 'Sandringhams' rebuilt with a higher pressure boiler on the lines of the later 'B17/6s', with a tractive effort increased by 10% as a result. These would have been supplemented by members of the 'V4' class, despite their relatively small 5ft 8in coupled wheels, and it would have been of interest to have observed the performance of these engines on the 520 tons of the 'Hook Continental', for example.

Edward Thompson's postwar locomotive building programme envisaged nothing between the Class 5 (using BR power classification) of the 'B1s' and the Class 8 of his Pacifics. Of these, only the 'B1s' could be permitted on Great Eastern metals, until track relaying and final reconstruction of underline bridges had been completed. It was not until early BR days that the problem was recognised and adequate motive power made available — 13 of the first 15 Class 7 'Britannia' Pacifics, with a 20¼ ton axle load, being allocated to East Anglian sheds.

Of the large-wheeled LNER 4-6-0s, those with the highest tractive effort were the 'B3s', the 'B17s', and the Thompson rebuilds of the 'B2' and 'B3/3' classes. The first of these were the most powerful locomotives possessed by the LNER at the Grouping, apart from the two classes of Pacific, and had Robinson been appointed Chief Mechanical Engineer in 1923 (it will be recalled that he claimed to have been offered the post) there is the strong possibility that the locomotive world would have seen a development of the 'Lord Faringdon' class into something resembling Maunsell's 'Lord Nelson', or even a Pacific; a 4-6-2 is known to have been outlined, but based on a two-cylinder design. In its day, the 'B3' was a leading design amongst the 4-6-0s of the pre-Grouping railways; it is not easy to give the same prominence to Thompson's 'B2' and 'B3/3' rebuilds, which in effect were no more than 'B1s' with a larger wheel diameter. One would have thought that the resources applied to what were virtually replacements would have been better devoted to building a further 10 'B1s'.

The basis of comparison of two or more locomotive classes rests on more than one criterion: horsepower exerted, thermal efficiency and mechanical reliability are only three amongst several, and in any case, in the absence of a comprehensive locomotive testing station and extended road trials, few steps were taken to assess any of these scientifically. So far as indicated or drawbar horsepowers are concerned, some evidence was obtained from indicator diagrams, dynamometer car trials, or recorded performance. From such figures as have been published, many derived from the calculations of Gp Capt Law, it is clear that the Great Western 'Kings' (when fitted with

'B7' No 1360 is seen working a down Class 'A' freight passing Wortley station on the Woodhead route in June 1948.
Austin Brackenbury

Right:
No 1306 *Mayflower* can be seen on the Great Central Railway at Loughborough, where it is ready to leave the station yard with a mail train on 13 June 1982.
A. D. M. Clay

double chimneys) and the rebuilt 'Royal Scots' of the LMS, both with the ability to exceed 2,000ihp were well ahead of other 4-6-0s in terms of power output. However, a steam locomotive is only capable of giving its maximum output when in good condition, with a good crew and good coal. There is a wealth of difference between the performance of (say) No 61251 when in prime condition on the 1948 interchange trials, and a similar locomotive with 60,000 miles since it was last in shops, and with the tender full of briquettes and coal dust.

Of the LNER classes, the normal maximum for a 'B1' or a 'B17' was a little over 1,500ihp, and for the 'B12/3', 1,450ihp. The latter were the most powerful inside-cylinder 4-6-0s to have been employed on a British railway, the 'Cardeans' or the LNWR 'Princes' achieving a normal maximum of around 1,200ihp. Of course, a larger 4-6-0, of say 1,800ihp would have been feasible, but neither Doncaster nor NBL could have designed one light enough to travel the Great Eastern in 1928. However, something on these lines could have been attempted as part of Thompson's postwar programme, in 1945, when track improvements had been made and Great Eastern traffic requirements called for something more than a 'B1'.

Investigation of the performance characteristics of the LNER 4-6-0s indicate that some could show a surprising turn of speed. Recordings of train timings must rely on the skill of the observer, and human error is a consideration in a study of exceptional performances, particularly if one is *willing* an engine to achieve something special! However, information from reputable sources demonstrates that whilst no LNER 4-6-0 is known to have reached the 'ton', a number have achieved over 90mph. The palm seems to lie with a pair of 'B1s', Nos 61326 and 61087, which notched up no less than 94mph at Ruddington, just south of Nottingham, with 360 tons. What manner of enginemen these were, and what their motivation was, is not recorded. A pair of 'B17s' on the 6.20pm from Marylebone reached 92mph near Whetstone, whilst 90mph was fairly frequently attained by 'B17s' on this train, and the down 'Newspaper'. Cecil J. Allen has described a prewar run with a 'B12/3' (referred to in more detail in Appendix III) in which 90mph was touched near Diss, and others of the older engines were timed at 85-86mph on the Great Central and Great Eastern, and on the Great Northern when the 'B3s' were on the Pullmans; Caprotti 'B3/2s' are known to have reached 88mph. The 'B7s' and 'B16s' were recorded at 77mph, and probably the rebuilt 'B16s' could have travelled faster but no recordings have been traced.

As a final commentary, it is fair to say that although the pioneer 4-6-0s of the North Eastern and Great Central Railways did not last long on the work for which they were intended, they made a leading contribution to the development of the type in Great Britain. Moreover, the two multi-cylinder mixed traffic classes of these two railways were nominally the most powerful designs of their kind to have been produced.

In his 'B1', Edward Thompson brought together a number of Gresley features, allied to his own standardised concept of two outside cylinders, resulting in what was to be almost the last new locomotive design in the classic British style, with a minimum of external pipes and protuberances. Many may regret the non-appearance of a Gresley equivalent of a 'Castle', but it is clear that after the success of the 'V2s' no need existed for such a locomotive.

It is fortunate that two class 'B1s' have survived, along with a 'B12/3', although we must regret that posterity has been denied the opportunity to savour the sight and sound of one of John G. Robinson's four-cylinder classes, or, in an unrebuilt 'B16', an example of the final Raven style. The LNER family of 4-6-0s represented a rich cross-section of a breed which provided the workhorses of many services — both passenger and freight — across the entire LNER system, and offers a fertile field for yet further study.

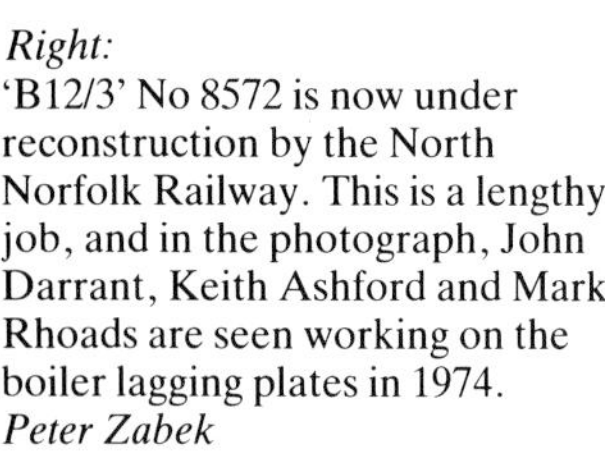

Right:
'B12/3' No 8572 is now under reconstruction by the North Norfolk Railway. This is a lengthy job, and in the photograph, John Darrant, Keith Ashford and Mark Rhoads are seen working on the boiler lagging plates in 1974.
Peter Zabek

Appendix I
Names and Numbers

Locomotive Numbering

Class	*Pre-Grouping Nos*	*LNER Nos**	*Post-1946 LNER/BR Nos†*
B1‡	195/196	5195/5196	1479/80
B2§	423-428	5423-5428	1490-93
B3	1164-1169	6164-6169	1494-98
B4	1095-1104	6095-6104	1481-89
B5	180-187, 1067-1072	5180-5187, 6067-6072	1678-90
B6	52/53, 416	5052/53, 54126	1346-48
B7	31-38, 72/73/78, 458-474	5031-5038, 5072/3/8, 5458-5474	1360-97 (survivors renumbered 61702-7/9-13 in 1949)
B8	4, 279/80, 439-446	5004, 5279/80, 5439-46	1349-59
B9	1105-1114	6105-6114	1469-78
B12	1500-1570	8500-05/07-80	1500-05/07-80
B13	726, 738-41/3-63/6, 768/75, 1077, 2001-10	Unchanged plus 2366-82, 1371-85	1699
B14	2111-2115	Unchanged	—
B15	782/6-8/91/5-9, 813/5/7/9-25	Unchanged	1693-5-7
B16	840-9, 906/8/9/11/4/5, 920-34/6/7/42/3/ 2363-5	Unchanged	1400-68 (61400-9 renumbered 61469-78 in 1949)
B17	—	2800-2872	1600-72
B1	—	8301-8310	1000-1287, E1288-E1303, 61304-61409

* Including locomotives built after Grouping to earlier designs.
† The 1946 renumbering was based on date order of construction and did not necessarily follow the earlier numerical sequence. A few engines had interim LNER numbers. Add 60000 for BR numbers where applicable.
‡ Later 'B18'.
§ Later 'B19'.

Right:
The nameplate of 'B17' No 61652 *Darlington*, photographed at Cambridge on 7 June 1958.
Ian Allan Library

Named Locomotives

Class B1

1000	*Springbok*
1001	*Eland*
1002	*Impala*
1003	*Gazelle*
1004	*Oryx*
1005	*Bongo*
1006	*Blackbuck*
1007	*Klipspringer*
1008	*Kudu*
1009	*Hartebeeste*
1010	*Wildebeeste*
1011	*Waterbuck*
1012	*Puku*
1013	*Topi*
1014	*Oribi*
1015	*Duiker*
1016	*Inyala*
1017	*Bushbuck*
1018	*Gnu*
1019	*Nilghai*
1020	*Gemsbok*
1021	*Reitbok*
1022	*Sassaby*
1023	*Hirola*
1024	*Addax*
1025	*Pallah*
1026	*Ourebi*
1027	*Madoqua*
1028	*Umseke*
1029	*Chamois*
1030	*Nyala*
1031	*Reedbuck*
1032	*Stembok*
1033	*Dibatag*
1034	*Chiru*
1935	*Pronghorn*
1036	*Ralph Assheton*
1037	*Jairou*
1038	*Blacktail*
1039	*Steinbok*
1040	*Roedeer*
1189	*Sir William Gray*
1215	*William Henton Carver*
1221	*Sir Alexander Erskine-Hill*
1237	*Geoffrey H. Kitson*
1238	*Leslie Runciman*
1240	*Harry Hinchcliffe*
1241	*Viscount Ridley*
1242	*Alexander Reith Gray*
1243	*Sir Harold Mitchell*
1244	*Strang Steel*
1245	*Murray of Elibank*
1246	*Lord Balfour of Burleigh*
1247	*Lord Burghley*
1248	*Geoffrey Gibbs*
1249	*Fitzherbert Wright*
1250	*A. Harold Bibby*
1251	*Oliver Bury*
61379	*Mayflower* (July 1951)

Class B2, later Class B19

5423	1490	*Sir Sam Fay*
5424	—	*City of Lincoln*
5425	1491	*City of Manchester*
5426	—	*City of Chester*
5427	1492	*City of London*
5428	1493	*City of Liverpool*

Name removed from No 5427 September 1937.

Class B3

6169	1494	*Lord Faringdon*
6164	1495	*Earl Beatty*
6165	1496	*Valour*
6166	1497	*Earl Haig*
6167	1498	*Lloyd George*
6168	—	*Lord Stuart of Wortley*

Name removed from No 6166 October 1943 when rebuilt as Class B3/3.
Name removed from No 6167 August 1923.

Class B4

6097	1482	*Immingham*

Class B8

5004	1349	*Glenalmond*
5439	1350	*Sutton Nelthorpe*
5446	1357	*Earl Roberts of Kandahar*
5279	1358	*Earl Kitchener of Khartoum*

Class B17

2800	1600	*Sandringham*
2801	1601	*Holkham*
2802	1602	*Walsingham*
2803	1603	*Framlingham*
2804	1604	*Elveden*
2805	1605	*Burnham Thorpe*
2806	1606	*Audley End*
2807	1607	*Blickling*
2808	1608	*Gunton*
2809	1609	*Quidenham*
2810	1610	*Honingham Hall*
2811	1611	*Raynham Hall*
2812	1612	*Houghton Hall*
2813	1613	*Woodbastwick Hall*
2814	1614	*Castle Hedingham*
2815	1615	*Culford Hall*
2816	1616	*Fallodon*
2817	1617	*Ford Castle*
2818	1618	*Wynyard Park*
2819	1619	*Welbeck Abbey*
2820	1620	*Clumber*
2821	1621	*Hatfield House*
2822	1622	*Alnwick Castle*
2823	1623	*Lambton Castle*
2824	1624	*Lumley Castle*
2825	1625	*Raby Castle*
2826	1626	*Brancepeth Castle*
2827	1627	*Aske Hall*
2828	1628	*Harewood House*
2829	1629	*Naworth Castle*
2830	1630	*Thoresby Park*
2831	1631	*Serlby Hall*
2832	1632	*Belvoir Castle*
2833	1633	*Kimbolton Castle*
2834	1634	*Hinchingbrooke*
2835	1635	*Milton*
2836	1636	*Harlaxton Manor*
2837	1637	*Thorpe Hall*
2838	1638	*Melton Hall*
2839	1639	*Rendelsham Hall*
2840	1640	*Somerleyton Hall*
2841	1641	*Gayton Hall*
2842	1642	*Kilverstone Hall*
2843	1643	*Champion Lodge*
2844	1644	*Earlham Hall*
2845	1645	*The Suffolk Regiment*
2846	1646	*Gilwell Park*
2847	1647	*Helmingham Hall*
2848	1648	*Arsenal*
2849	1649	*Sheffield United*
2850	1650	*Grimsby Town*
2851	1651	*Derby County*
2852	1652	*Darlington*
2853	1653	*Huddersfield Town*
2854	1654	*Sunderland*
2855	1655	*Middlesbrough*
2856	1656	*Leeds United*
2857	1657	*Doncaster Rovers*
2858	1658	*Newcastle United*
2859	1659	*Norwich City*
2860	1660	*Hull City*
2861	1661	*Sheffield Wednesday*
2862	1662	*Manchester United*
2863	1663	*Everton*
2864	1664	*Liverpool*
2865	1665	*Leicester City*
2866	1666	*Nottingham Forest*
2867	1667	*Bradford*
2868	1668	*Bradford City*
2869	1669	*Barnsley*
2870	1670	*Manchester City*
2871	1671	*Manchester City*
2872	1672	*West Ham United*

No 2803 rebuilt B2 October 1946.
No 2805 renamed *Lincolnshire Regiment* April 1938.
No 2807 rebuilt B2 May 1947.
No 2814 rebuilt B2 November 1946.
No 2815 rebuilt B2 September 1946.
No 2816 rebuilt B2 November 1945
No 2817 rebuilt December 1946.
No 2830 renamed *Tottenham Hotspur* January 1938.
No 2832 rebuilt B2 July 1947; renamed *Royal Sovereign* October 1958.
No 2839 renamed *Norwich City* January 1938; rebuilt B2 January 1946.
No 2844 rebuilt B2 March 1949.
No 2858 renamed *The Essex Regiment* June 1936.
No 2859 renamed *East Anglian* and streamlined September 1937.
No 2870 renamed *Tottenham Hotspur* May 1937; renamed *City of London* and streamlined September 1937.
No 2871 rebuilt B2 August 1945; renamed *Royal Sovereign* April 1946.

Right:
The nameplate of streamlined 'B17' No 2859 *East Anglian*.
A. Swain

Appendix II
Principal Dimensions

The dimensions in this table are those which applied during most of the LNER period. Minor differences occurred within the lifetime of a class, for example, the tyres of the earliest Great Central 4-6-0s were later increased in thickness by 1in. Where older engines were subsequently provided with superheated boilers, the dimensions shown are those after superheating. Figures of tractive effort may differ from those published elsewhere, but all have been recalculated on the basis of 85% boiler pressure.

Class		*Cylinders diam (in)*	*Cylinders stroke (in)*	*Coupled wheels (ft in)*	*Boiler pressure (lb/sq in)*	*Heating surface (sq ft)*	*Grate area (sq ft)*	*Tractive effort (lb)*
B1*	(2)	21	26	6 9	180	1,951	26.2	21,658
B1	(2)	20	26	6 2	225	2,005	27.9	26,878
B2†	(2)	20	26	6 9	180	2,387	26.5	19,644
B2	(2)	20	26	6 8	225	2,005	27.9	24,863
B3	(4)	16	26	6 9	180	2,387	26.5	25,145
B3/3	(2)	20	26	6 9	225	2,005	27.9	24,556
B4	(2)	19	26	6 7	180	1,951	26.2	18,178
B5	(2)	19	26	6 1	180	1,795	23.5	19,672
B6	(2)	21	26	5 8	180	2,123	26.3	25,799
B7	(4)	16	26	5 8	180	2,387	26.5	29,952
B8	(2)	21½	26	5 7	180	2,387	26.5	27,445
B9	(2)	19	26	5 4	180	1,951	23.8	22,438
B12	(ins)	20	28	6 6	180	1,834	26.5	21,969
B12/3	(ins)	20	28	6 6	180	1,874	31.0	21,969
B13	(2)	20	26	6 1¼	160	1,659	23.0	19,309
B14	(2)	20	26	6 8¼	175	1,750	23.0	19,277
B15	(2)	20	26	6 1¼	175	1,730	23.0	21,119
B16	(3)	18½	26	5 8	180	1,958	27.0	30,032
B17	(3)	17½	26	6 8	200	2,020	27.5	25,380
B17/6	(3)	17½	26	6 8	225	2,005	27.9	28,553

* Later 'B18'. † Later 'B19'.

GWR								
No 100	(2)	18	30	6 8	200	2,400	27.8	20,655
Hall	(2)	18½	30	6 0	225	2,033	27.1	27,273
Star	(4)	14¼	26	6 8½	225	2,143	27.0	25,086
LMS								
Cardean	(ins)	20	26	6 6	200	2,414	26.0	22,667
Prince	(ins)	20½	26	6 3	175	1,952	25.0	21,670
Claughton	(4)	16	26	6 9	175	2,403	30.5	24,446
Jubilee	(3)	17	26	6 9	225	1,852	29.5	26,612
Class 5	(2)	18½	28	6 0	225	1,844	27.8	25,455
Southern								
H15	(2)	21	28	6 0	180	2,216	30.0	26,240

Appendix III
Comparative Performance

The comparative performance of locomotives is a subject which should be approached with caution, as, apart from the question of accuracy of the recordings, there are variables such as the engine's condition, the attitude of its crew, increased loads, altered schedules and changing permanent way conditions, so that it is not often possible to compare like with like.

However, with this caveat, it is of interest to examine the information which is available about the LNER 4-6-0s. This centres primarily on the main lines of the Great Central and the Great Eastern, as on each of these, three generations of locomotives — the pre-Grouping classes, Gresley's 'B17s' and Thompson's 'B1s' — may be reviewed. Relatively few recordings seem to have been compiled of journeys behind 4-6-0s of various classes on other parts of the LNER system, or on goods trains. This is perhaps because of lack of opportunity — (it was virtually impossible for example for the average person to travel on the engine or in the guard's van of a freight train) — or because journeys were considered unworthy of recording, or were spoiled by out-of-course checks. Moreover, although there is a good deal of photographic evidence of the GCR 4-6-0s at work on the early LNER Pullman trains, and on excursions such as Eason's Specials, little seems to have been preserved of their performance on these trains. The same applies to the Great North of Scotland and the subsidiary lines of the North Eastern, where locomotive output did not often have to reach very high levels, although undoubtedly many sterling performances went unrecorded. On the North British, too, there is a dearth of records, but the opportunity for the 'B1s' to shine would have been present as substitutes for larger locomotives on the main lines radiating from Edinburgh, as well as in lesser services in their own right.

Most of the logs in the tables which follow are reproduced by courtesy of the Editor of the *Railway Magazine*. All train weights are in gross tons. One of the fastest turns on the Great Central line was the precisely timed 2.32am from Marylebone, on which a Neasden locomotive worked through to Leicester. Here, engines were changed, so that a fresh locomotive took over for the brief 60mph dash to Arkwright Street, Nottingham. The train was primarily made up of newspaper vans, with one Brake Composite for passengers, and having regard to the unsocial hours during which the train ran it is not surprising that few recorders travelled on it. However, R. Dyson did so in May 1929, behind a 'B3', as did O. S. Nock in 1935 with a 'B17'. The load was significantly greater on the second run.

2.32am Marylebone to Leicester via Aylesbury

Locomotive:		'B3' No 6168			'B17' No 2841		
Load:		220 tons			300 tons		
Distance		*Schedule*	*Actual*	*Speed*	*Schedule*	*Actual*	*Speed*
miles		*min*	*min*	*mph*	*min*	*min*	*mph*
0.0	Marylebone	0	0.00	—	0	0.00	—
5.1	Neasden S Jn	9		68	8½	8.32	70½
9.2	Harrow-on-the-Hill	13	12.45	45	12½	12.34	53
16.1	Watford S Jn*	20	20.10	65	19	19.11	75½
23.6	Amersham		31.20	40		31.50	36
37.9	Aylesbury	44	45.00	64½	43	44.15	
44.4	Quainton Rd Jn	52	51.20	57½	50	49.26	56
59.3	Brackley	67	67.20		66	64.45	
9.8	Woodford	10	11.50	63	11½	11.27	72½
23.9	Rugby	24	24.25		25½	23.46	
15.2	Whetstone		15.35	83½		14.45	90
19.9	Leicester Central	20	19.50		20	19.02	

*Severe service slack at Rickmansworth

Until April 1937 the 3.20pm down Manchester was headed on alternate days by Neasden and Gorton locomotives working through, after which Gorton took over entirely. The train was allowed 109min non-stop to Leicester, compared with the 111min of the 2.32am with two stops. Two runs with GCR 4-6-0s may be set against one in 1938 with a 'B17', hauling a heavier train. The 4.55pm down Manchester was an easier task, as although the schedule allowed 1min less to Leicester, the load was no more than five bogies when the train was timed behind No 6164.

Left:
Headed by 'B3' No 6165 *Valour* the 3.20pm Marylebone-Manchester is seen leaving the London terminus in LNER days.
F. E. Mackay

Marylebone to Leicester via Aylesbury

Locomotive:			No 6164		No 2862		No 5427		No 6164
Load:			300 tons		360 tons		235 tons		185 tons
Distance		*Schedule*	*Actual*	*Speed*	*Actual*	*Speed*	*Actual*	*Schedule*	*Actual*
miles		*min*	*min*	*mph*	*min*	*mph*	*min*	*min*	*min*
0.0	Marylebone	0	0.00	—	0.00	—	0.00	0	0.00
5.1	Neasden S Jn	9	9.40	62½	9.15	37½		8½	7.35
9.2	Harrow	14	14.20	46½	13.27	37½	14.04	13	11.45
17.2	Rickmansworth*	23	22.50		21.48	37½	23.40	22	20.30
23.6	Amersham		33.10	36	32.44	33½	30.40	45	28.35
37.9	Aylesbury	46	47.30		46.27	60	46.07	45	41.45
44.1	Quainton Rd	52½	53.30		52.12	64	51.41	52	47.30
59.3	Brackley		69.00	66.22		67.29		63.40	
69.1	Woodford	77	79.00		75.47		79.32	76	73.55
78.5	Braunston		87.40		84.07	80	85.32		82.35
83.2	Rugby		92.05	88.11		89.32		86.40	
									pws
98.4	Whetstone		106.00			103.17		98.05	
			sigs	eased					
103.1	Leicester	109	111.55	—	107.42	—	107.30	108	106.28

*Severe service slack

Fewer runs seem to have been recorded in the up direction between Leicester and Marylebone, but one which has reached the archives is of an unchecked run in early LNER days. A 'B2' still bearing its GCR number reached Marylebone in 109¼min with 265 tons, but Cecil J. Allen compared its performance rather unfavourably with that of a 'Director' hauling a similar load. The second run in the table below represents probably the ultimate performance by a 'B17', when on a Saturday in July 1939 No 2848 headed the 8.51am up from Leicester and lost only 1min to Marylebone on a run checked by a permanent way slack near Harrow. Normally the train was made up of nine bogies, but it was strengthened on this occasion by a further four coaches working through from a boat arrival at Immingham. The 109min schedule represented an average speed of 56.75mph.

Non-stop running to Leicester ceased in the postwar era, and even the 'Master Cutler' stopped at Rugby. A record of No 61116 on an aggregate 139min schedule with four stops indicates that even with 395 tons behind the tender the engine had something in hand, and some sectional timings were faster than those of No 2848. However, the 'B1' had the opportunity to recover boiler pressure and water level during the stops.

Leicester to Marylebone via Aylesbury

Locomotive:		'B2' No 427**		'B17' No 2848			'B1' No 61116		
Load:		265 tons		465 tons			395 tons		
Distance		*Actual*	*Speed*	*Schedule*	*Actual*	*Speed*	*Schedule*	*Actual*	*Speed*
miles		*min*	*mph*	*min*	*min*	*mph*	*min*	*min*	*mph*
0.0	Leicester	0.00	—	0	0.00	—	0	0.00	—
4.7	Whetstone	6.53			7.45	50		7.04	57
19.9	Rugby	23.07	64		25.12	63	25	22.33	
34.0	Woodford	38.00		37	39.53	69½	20	19.58	
43.8	Brackley	47.06			48.46	79		11.22	79
59.0	Quainton Rd	59.32		59	61.14	71	23½	24.23	57
65.2	Aylesbury	65.55	65	65	66.37	69	34½	30.30	
79.5	Amersham	82.19	53		82.33	55		21.45	49
85.9	Rickmansworth*	88.56	65½	87½	88.11	80	30	28.13	71
93.9	Harrow	98.27	pws		98.47	pws	44	40.27	sigs
98.0	Neasden S Jn	102.42		101½	103.12	68	5½	6.32	sigs
103.1	Marylebone	109.17	—	109	110.06	—	15	17.30	—

*Severe service slack
**Schedule believed to have been 112min

The Woodhead route presented difficult working conditions, but around 1930 loads were light and schedules not over-onerous. However, few recordings appear to have been made, and most of these include scheduled stops and signal checks, making comparison difficult. The following table gives an example of an early 'Sandringham' turn on the initial stage of the seven-coach 'North Country Continental', departing from Manchester Central at 3.05pm, and following the circuitous route via Fallowfield to Guide Bridge. The locomotive suffered an early permanent way slowing, from which it did not fully recover.

Manchester Central to Sheffield Victoria

Locomotive:	'B17' No 2807		
Load:	240 tons		
Distance		*Schedule*	*Actual*
miles		*min*	*min*
0.0	Manchester Central	0	0.00
			pws
11.1	Guide Bridge	17	20.10
18.0	Dinting		29.45
25.3	Woodhead	39	41.30
28.5	Dunford Bridge	44	47.20
34.5	Penistone	51	54.05
42.5	Oughty Bridge		62.50
			sig stop
47.4	Sheffield Victoria	66	70.00

Typically, around 1930, at Sheffield the load was reduced to five coaches, and after a stop at Worksop, the connecting portion from York (including a through coach from Glasgow) was added at Lincoln, where 12min were allowed. The train then halted at Spalding, March, Ely and Bury St Edmunds, before arriving at Ipswich at 8.43pm. The 4-6-0 which had worked through from Manchester was then replaced, generally by a 'Claud Hamilton' 4-4-0, for the final 20.1 miles to Parkeston Quay, reached at 9.18pm. Aggregate journey time from Manchester, including stops, was 6hr 13min, representing an overall average speed of 43.1mph. The down train left Parkeston at 7.25am, arriving at Manchester at 2.17pm and Liverpool at 3.00pm. The timings, and the stops, varied from time to time.

Sheffield Victoria to Manchester London Road

Locomotive:		'B7' No 5072		'B17' No 2834			'B17' No 2858	
Load:		180 tons		180 tons			360 tons	
Distance		*Schedule*	*Actual*	*Schedule*	*Actual*	*Speed*	*Actual*	*Speed*
miles		*min*	*min*	*min*	*min*	*mph*	*min*	*mph*
0.0	Sheffield Victoria	0	0.00	0	0.00	—	0.00	—
4.9	Oughty Bridge		8.15				9.35	39½
12.9	Penistone	20	18.50	19	17.43	47	21.20	45
18.9	Dunford Bridge	29	27.10	27	25.58	44	29.58	40
22.1	Woodhead	33	30.45	31	29.23	62½	33.59	
29.4	Dinting		37.30		36.33	68	40.49	68
			pws				pws	
36.3	Guide Bridge	50	47.40	47	45.12	43	50.14	
41.3	Manchester London Rd	59	55.20	55	52.14	—	57.11	—

In the reverse direction over the Pennines, a 'B7' with five coaches had time in hand on an unchecked run to London Road station. The train was the 4.55pm from Marylebone, which was to be withdrawn beyond Sheffield from the winter of 1938. The load was then normally six coaches, but one had been removed as defective on the first of the two 'B17' runs below. In the last run, the train was strengthened to 10 coaches to cater for holiday traffic.

There is a general consensus that the hardest work on the Great Eastern section was on the down 'Hook Continental'. Not many records of these runs have survived, but one of the finest was recorded by Cecil J. Allen in pre-Grouping days, when the original 'B12s' were allowed no more than 82min with a train which could gross over 400 tons. This is contrasted with an early run on the 'Flushing Continental' by one of the first batch of 'Sandringhams', when the timing was 85min. The signal check suffered by the latter cost over 2min in the running, to which must be added a permanent way slack in the early stages. The third run took place after the 'Hook Continental' schedule had been eased to 87min, but the load was greater.

No records can be traced of *up* journeys, when the Continental passenger might be expected to look for a fast run to town. But with rush hour congestion virtually all the way to Liverpool Street, unchecked arrivals would have been very few.

In LNER days, the best regular times on the main line to Norwich were achieved in the two years before September 1939 by the 'East Anglian' express, which stopped briefly at Ipswich. Column 4 of the following table gives the record of the two parts of the run on separate occasions, the remainder in each case having been affected by checks. In early 1932, 'B17' No 2800 took part in test trips to and from Norwich to examine the possibilities for faster trains (Col 3), and runs by 'B12s' — again the two parts of the journey are shown separately — demonstrate their ability, in both unrebuilt and rebuilt form (Col 1). Finally, in BR days Great Eastern services were accelerated and runs are included in which a 'B1' is featured (Col 2), and a 'Britannia' Pacific (Col 5) shows what might have been done had the LNER provided the section with locomotives it deserved. The table is arranged, not in chronological order, but in order of speed.

Liverpool Street to Norwich via Ipswich

		(1)		(2)		(3)		(4)		(5)	
Distance		*Time*	*Speed*	*Time*	*Speed*	*Time*	*Speed*	*Time*	*Speed*	*Time*	*Speed*
miles		*min*	*mph*	*min*	*mph*	*min*	*mph*	*min*	*mph*	*min*	*mph*
0.0	Liverpool Street	0.00		0.00		0.00		0.00		0.00	
1.1	Bethnal Green					3.20	22**	3.28			
4.0	Stratford*	8.30		10.05		9.20	33†	7.35		7.35	
10.0	Chadwell Heath	15.55		19.08		16.24	60	15.50		13.54	
19.3	Ingrave SB	29.45	24½	32.50		26.12	39	27.48		23.38	
29.7	Chelmsford*	40.35	64	43.53	64	35.27	78	37.05	80	33.02	76
38.6	Witham	50.15	67	52.58	—	44.45	71	45.40	77	41.21	75
51.7	Colchester*	65.00		66.45		60.41	56	56.55	77½	53.20	72
59.5	Manningtree	73.50		75.40	74½	68.22	80	65.20		62.20	83
68.7	Ipswich	87.05	—	85.13	—	76.53	—	76.40	—	71.10	—
11.9	Stowmarket	13.35	72	15.16	61	12.40	70	11.50	75	13.17	72
26.3	Diss	25.59	90*	29.28	77	25.05	78	23.35	81	24.43	90
35.4	Forncett	40.26+	74	37.32		32.52	69	30.52	78½	31.36	
46.3	Norwich	52.29	—	51.09	—	44.40	—	42.00	—	41.50	—

(1) 'B12' No 8501 to Ipswich, load 470 tons, 90min schedule; 'B12/3' No 8535 to Norwich, 305 tons. Out-of-course stop at Diss.
(2) 'B1' No 1042, load 410 tons, to Ipswich, 85min schedule; 'B1' No 1048 on to Norwich, load 300 tons, 51min schedule.
(3) 'B17' No 2800 on trial run, load 295 tons. Out-of-course stop at Stanway box, 55min 47sec.
(4) 'B17/5s' No 2859 to Ipswich (80min schedule) and No 2870 to Norwich (48min). Both with 230 tons.
(5) BR No 70007, 330 tons. Schedule 73min to Ipswich, then 45min to Norwich. (NB: Two separate journeys).
*Speeds are as recorded just before restrictions or stops at these points
**Permanent way slack after this point
†Signal check after this point

Liverpool Street to Parkeston Quay

Locomotive:		'B12' No 1566			'B17' No 2804**		'B17' No 2805†	
Load:		415 tons			355 tons		465 tons	
Distance		*Schedule*	*Actual*	*Speed*	*Actual*	*Speed*	*Actual*	*Speed*
miles		*min*	*min*	*mph*	*min*	*mph*	*min*	*mph*
0.0	Liverpool Street	0	0.00	—	0.00	—	0.00	—
1.1	Bethnal Green		3.25		3.05		3.47	
4.0	Stratford*	8	7.50	40	8.34		8.42	53
10.0	Chadwell Heath	15	14.50	55	16.05		16.56	
			sigs					
19.3	Ingrave SB		26.25	33	27.30	30½	29.27	23½
29.7	Chelmsford*	38	36.30	55	37.50	70½	40.02	
38.6	Witham	48	45.35	66	47.05	65	49.03	69
					sigs			
51.7	Colchester*	61	58.25	50	61.55		61.45	45
59.5	Manningtree*	70	67.20	67	70.50	72	eased	
68.9	Parkeston Quay	82	80.15	—	83.20	—	86.06	—

*Speeds were recorded just before speed restrictions at these points
**Schedule 85min
†Schedule 87min

Because of the generally slower schedules of the earlier postwar period, the 'B1s' were not featured in any fast runs which could have been at all comparable with those of prewar days. Later, when matters had eased, larger locomotives were available for the most arduous workings, and the class did not have the opportunity to enter the limelight. This makes the appearance of No 61251 in the 1948 interchanges all the more interesting, and among its best performances were those on the Great Western main line between Plymouth and Bristol. From these, the following has been selected to demonstrate its capability with a 475-ton load — surely a 'Castle', if not a 'King' — size task — on the 44.8 miles from Taunton to Bristol, on 7 July 1948. A similar performance was given in the reverse direction, including a minimum of 47mph on Wellington Bank, when the engine was exerting around 1,500ihp; this must be regarded as one of the best performances ever by an LNER 4-6-0.

GWR Taunton to Bristol

Locomotive:	'B1' No 61251			
Load:	475 tons			
Distance		*Schedule*	*Actual*	*Speed*
miles		*min*	*min*	*mph*
0.0	Taunton	0	0.00	—
2.4	Creech Jn	4	4.20	56½
			sigs	
5.8	Durston		8.28	53
11.6	Bridgwater		14.40	57
14.1	Dunball		17.08	63
17.9	Highbridge	20	20.49	58
20.6	Brent Knoll		23.42	60
25.1	Uphill Jn	28	28.04	62
28.0	Worle Jn	31	30.49	64
32.8	Yatton		35.20	67
36.7	Nailsea		38.48	66
38.9	Flax Bourton		40.53	56
41.6	Long Ashton		sigs	eased
43.8	Bedminster		47.23	
			sigs	
44.8	Bristol Temple Meads	53	50.40	—

The engine gained 2½min on the 53min schedule, at an average speed of 53.2mph. However, the signal checks were estimated to have cost 5min in running time, so that had the run been unchecked a net time of 45½min would have been expected, giving an overall speed of 59mph.

The longest 4-6-0 workings on the Great Northern main line were between King's Cross and Grimsby. Here are an inward journey from Peterborough by a 'B3' on a 1930s excursion train, which Cecil Allen considered to be of the 'best Pacific quality' (until the run was ruined by signal checks) and a down run by a 'B1' 20 years later, with an Immingham driver working home, which reached 88mph at Three Counties.

Peterborough North to King's Cross

Locomotive: 'B3' No 6169
Load: 460 tons

Distance miles		*Time min*	*Speed mph*
0.0	Peterborough	0.00	—
7.0	Holme	9.50	65
12.9	Abbots Ripton	16.20	49
17.5	Huntingdon	20.25	70½
24.7	St Neots	26.50	62½
32.3	Sandy	33.45	78
35.3	Biggleswade	36.35	56
44.5	Hitchin	46.15	50
47.8	Stevenage	50.50	43
51.4	Knebworth	55.10	
58.7	Hatfield	62.35	
63.7	Potters Bar	69.00	sigs
71.4	Wood Green	80.15	sigs
73.9	Finsbury Park	84.35	sigs
76.4	King's Cross	89.45	—

King's Cross to Peterborough North

Locomotive: 'B1' No 61190
Load: 410 tons

Distance miles		*Schedule min*	*Actual min*	*Speed mph*
0.0	King's Cross	0	0.00*	—
2.5	Finsbury Park		8.02	33
5.0	Wood Green		11.30	52
12.7	Potters Bar	20	21.13	47½
17.7	Hatfield	27	26.12*	66
28.6	Stevenage		37.40	59¼
31.9	Hitchin		42.29	78
41.1	Biggleswade		49.07	80½
44.2	Sandy	52	51.26	76
47.5	Tempsford		54.10	74
51.7	St Neots		57.47	72
58.9	Huntingdon	65	65.30	
69.4	Holme		79.32*	
76.4	Peterborough	92	88.05	—

*Permanent way slacks after these points

An example of good non-stop work is provided by No 61061, working an advance portion of the 'North Briton' between Newcastle and Edinburgh:

Newcastle Central to Edinburgh Waverley

Locomotive: 'B1' No 61061
Load: 255 tons

Distance miles		*Actual min*	*Speed mph*
—	Newcastle	0.00	—
16.6	Morpeth*	22.07	38
34.9	Alnmouth	39.19	67
51.7	Belford	55.06	68
67.0	Berwick*	68.36	40
95.3	Dunbar	96.10	72
		sigs, pws	
124.5	Edinburgh	140.29	—

*Service slack

A typical 'B1' duty in the North Eastern Area was between York and Hull; here, in the reverse direction, is a record of 'B1' No 1010 *Wildebeeste* on the stopping train leaving Hull at 3.10pm. A top speed of 76mph was checked by signals before Stamford Bridge.

Hull to York

Locomotive: 'B1' No 1010
Load: 200 tons

Distance miles		*Schedule min*	*Actual min*	*Speed mph*
—	Hull	0	—	—
8.3	Beverley	12	—	—
11.4	Market Weighton	17	15.05	
6.4	Pocklington	11	8.55	
			sigs	76
6.5	Stamford Bridge		7.45	
10.0	Warthill		10.27	
13.6	Earswick		13.45	
			sig stop	
16.1	York	23	19.30	

In the Northern Scottish Area, the main 'B12' working in the late 1930s was the 7.50am from Aberdeen, which conveyed the through coaches off the previous evening's 7.25pm from King's Cross. This arrived at Inverness via Craigellachie at 11.34am, after nine intermediate stops. The longest stage was between Aberdeen and Huntly, 57min being allowed for the 44.4 miles. The best train along the Deeside line was the 5.05pm from Aberdeen, allowed 24min for the 16¾ miles to Banchory. After a further four stops, Ballater (43¼ miles) was reached at 6.17pm.

Appendix IV
Coal Consumption

Statistics of the coal consumption of LNER classes were prepared from regularly collected records of the coal issued to locomotives and their mileage. These were classified by locomotive class and area, but not divided into sub-classes, so that there is no similar information to compare for example the 'B12/1' with the 'B12/3', although special tests took place on occasion. The figures in the following table are the average for the four years 1936-39. However, the figures must be approached with caution, as they do not have regard for the weight of the trains hauled, and would have been better had they been on the basis of *ton*-miles, ie taking note of the weight of the trains. In any case, locomotive design is only one factor in coal/mile figures; operating methods are a further influence — engines engaged in freight service for example wasting more coal standing still than express passenger engines. Another important aspect is the effect of the generally lower calorific value of the coal used in Scotland, which had the effect of increasing the weight of coal burned by as much as 10%, for the same output.

Nevertheless, some interesting conclusions may be drawn. The 'B17s' were used more intensively on the Great Central than on the Great Eastern and achieved a higher fuel efficiency. This suggests that the average loadings must have been higher on the GE than on the GC, although speeds were higher on the latter. Also, the similarity is remarkable between the performance of the 'B2s' and the 'B3s'.

Of the mixed traffic classes, there is a similarity between the 'B7s' and the Gresley 'K3' 2-6-0s, but the Raven 'B16s' in their unrebuilt form were not only used less intensively, but also appeared heavier on coal. Perhaps their lower aggregate mileage was a factor in their retention in service after the 'B7s' had been withdrawn.

Class		*Average miles per year*	*Coal consumption lb/mile*
B1	(later B18)	26,411	52.6
B2	(later B19)	44,180	54.5
B3		44,110	54.7
B4		29,071	55.4
B5		34,045	55.3
B6		32,905	60.6
B7		37,870	61.8
B8		26,933	67.8
B9		25,211	62.2
B12	(GE Section)	39,911	55.7
	(Scottish Area)	32,441	63.3
B13	(1936-38)	11,873	75.1
B15		23,362	63.2
B16		28,514	63.9
B17	(GC Section)	57,460	44.7
	(GE Section)	41,109	54.1
K3	(GN Section)	37,327	60.4

Based on information prepared by J. Cliffe from original LNER records.

Right:
'B16' No 61429 climbs away from Bardsley with a returning Leeds City-Wetherby race special in 1961. *J. M. Rayner*

Index

BRITISH RAILWAYS
61565